Some books are to be tasted,
others to be swallowed,
and some few to be chewed and digested.

Sir Francis Bacon

More Learning in Less Time

A guide
*for students, professionals, career-changers,
and lifelong learners*

FIFTH EDITION

Norma B. Kahn
M.S., M.A., Ed.D.

Ways-to Books, Inc.
Gwynedd Valley, Pennsylvania

Ways-to Books, Inc.
Post Office Box 167
Gwynedd Valley, PA 19437-0167

Library of Congress Catalog Card Number: 98-60706

ISBN 0-9664353-0-3

Cover and typography by Hyland/Ocko Associates

Printing and binding by Thomson-Shore, Inc.

First and second printings, 1998

1   2

Contents

Part III: Ways to Improve Favorable Attitudes and Avoid Unfavorable Ones

Part IV: Ways to Read and Learn Well and with Pleasure – Lifelong

Preface to the fifth edition

For this fifth edition of *More Learning in Less Time*, I have
retained most of the fourth edition, updating and revising parts
of it, and I have added new material:

> — *information and advice about using computers, in
> chapter 9;*

> — *more recommendations about improving motivation, in
> chapter 16;*

> — *more advice about learning collaboratively as well as
> independently;*

> — *more examples of ways to apply basic principles or
> strategies to a variety of academic and professional
> assignments and responsibilities and to analogous
> activities;*

> — *a new section, "Solving problems in physics," in
> chapter 6;*

> — *two new chapters: What to Avoid: Self-Defeating
> Tendencies, chapter 17, and Getting More Pleasure from
> Reading, chapter 20;*

> — *another appendix, Progress in Helping Students Avoid
> Self-Defeating Tendencies.*

In working on this edition, I have thought of my readers as 1)
traditional-age undergraduates and graduate or professional students, 2) adults enrolled in continuing-education programs or
returning to formal education to prepare for new careers, and 3)
adults engaged continually in informal education. I have kept in
mind returning students especially, because half of all undergraduates now are age twenty-five or older, and many adults are
enrolled in long-distance courses in which they communicate
with their instructors and fellow students primarily by e-mail and
teleconferencing.

I wish all my benefactors and readers well as we continue to help
one another learn more, in less time, and with more joy.

Acknowledgments

As I recommend to others for appropriate work such as this, I used a collaborative process in writing *More Learning in Less Time*. I am also following my recommendations in acknowledging and thanking the many people who have given me information and advice for this edition and earlier editions. Many of the people I name below have been or are now on the faculty or staff of the University of Pennsylvania:

Professors and other Ph.D.s:

> *Education: Carol Brown, Myrna Cohen, Susan Lytle, and Margot Soven*
>
> *Foreign languages: Flora Cornfield and Barbara Freed*
>
> *History: Marvin Becker, Michael Katz, Mark Lytle, and Eric Schneider*
>
> *Law: Louis B. Schwartz*
>
> *Literature: Augusto Hacthoun, Edward B. Irving, Jr. (supervisor of my doctoral dissertation, "Design and Implementation of a High School Literature Program to Motivate Lifetime Reading of Literature")*
>
> *Management and business education: Diane Bradford and Connie Mullinix*
>
> *Math, science and technology: Adam Bernstein, Richard D. Paul, Bryan Roberts, David Shale, Paul Soven, and Roger Walmsley*
>
> *Psychology: Jonathan Baron and Joan Lerner*

Other professionals:

> *Attorneys: Marilyn T. Benjamin, Arthur Berger, Arthur Seidel, Alan Kahn, my husband, and James T. Kahn, our son*
>
> *Director of programs for returning students: Rhea Mandell*

Judicial officer: Lyn Davis

Librarians: John Kupersmith, Lauris Olson, Robert Persing, and Robert Walther

Editors:

Robert Boynton, of Boynton/Cook, editor/publisher of the first two editions of this book and author of Introduction to the Poem *(see chapter 7)*

George Young and Mariah Bear, of Ten Speed Press, which published the third and fourth editions

Bonnie Clause, who helped me polish this fifth edition for publication

Graphic designers:

Sharka Brod Hyland and Melissa Gable, of Hyland/Ocko Associates, who improved the visual appearance of the text and designed the cover, for publication by Ways-to Books, Inc.

I recognize my debt to the professors in my undergraduate and master's degree programs in English and my master's and doctoral degree programs in Education. I am also grateful to the scores of students, colleagues, friends, and family members who suggested subjects, sentences, and organizational modifications for this book.

The author and publisher wishes to thank the following who have kindly given permission for the use of copyright material:

Heinemann Boynton/Cook Publishers and Sandra Boynton for Sandra Boynton's illustration of the quotation from Sir Francis Bacon's "Of Studies"

Harry G. Henn and Practising Law Institute, for excerpts from *Henn on Copyright Law: A Practitioner's Guide*, 3rd ed., 1991

Leonard Miller, for his questionnaire about test anxiety, copyright © 1979

Viking Penguin, a division of Penguin Books USA, Inc., for the graphic representation of "Abraham Maslow's Hierarchy of Needs," from *The Third Force: The Psychology of Abraham Maslow*, by Frank Goble, which was published by Pocket Books in 1971, by arrangement with Grossman Publishers, Inc. Copyright © 1970 by Thomas Jefferson Research Center.

Every effort has been made to trace all the copyright holders, but if any has been overlooked the publishers will be pleased to make the necessary arrangements.

Although their work is beyond copyright, the excellent nineteenth-century artists of the London newspaper Punch deserve thanks for the illustrations that lighten this guidebook.

Finally, I express my appreciation of—if not to—Isaac Watts, the author of *Improvement of the Mind* (1741), whose astonishingly modern ideas and gracefully antique language enhance my pages and give them historical interest. Isaac Watts based his book in part on John Locke's *An Essay Concerning Human Understanding*, which was written in 1690 and was among the most widely read and influential books of the eighteenth century. Watts was a great English cleric and the author of many hymns still sung today, including "O God, Our Help in Ages Past" and "Joy to the World" – titles that express the feelings of many students and professionals at critical times.

Introduction

This is a "ways-to" book, more than a "how-to" one. It invites
you to try various ways to learn more in less time and to adapt
them according to your individual style and purposes. The book
is organized and formatted to help you understand it quickly.
Many sections are segmented and indented beyond usual para-
graphing to make the content that much clearer and more
memorable.

Why not start by looking through the table of contents, marking
the sections that most appeal to you, and completing the self-
evaluation? Then, start reading one of the sections that especially
interests you. Whatever order you choose for continued reading,
use a quick marking method in the table of contents and in the
margins of the sections. For example, use checks to remind yourself which sections you read and found interesting, and arrows to
remind yourself which sections or ideas you want to try applying.
(See chapter 18 for more detailed suggestions for marking tables
of contents, to make them records of your reading and guides
to action.)

More Learning in Less Time is designed as a guidebook, for
readers to consult according to their current needs rather than to
read from cover to cover. So, in many of the sections you'll find
a referral to another section that can give you more background,
if you need it to understand better the particular section you
chose to read.

If you are concerned about studying a subject not discussed
directly in this book, look for sections that seem applicable for
your purposes. For example, to study pharmacology read chapter
3, Remembering Effectively, and consider how you could apply
the principles or strategies to the material you have to learn.

Many of the sections of this book recommend a variation of four
basic strategies that are helpful in many kinds of reading, writing, and study, and in analogous activities. You'll also find several references to the centuries-old analogy of reading or knowledge to eating or nourishment, because that analogy is so useful

when you're trying to decide the best way to approach various activities or assignments.

The sooner you begin to read, write, and study more effectively and efficiently, the more you'll learn and remember – both for school and for purposes beyond school. Countless undergraduate, graduate, and professional-school students and many experienced professionals have told me that they wish they had known better ways to learn when they were in high school or their first year of college.

Developing an attitude that is both realistic and optimistic is also vital to academic success. Some first-year college students who were very successful in high school assume that college work will be no harder for them than high school work was, and so they make no attempt to improve the ways they study. When these students receive low grades for the first time, they find that the emotional effect interferes with their concentration. Improving their study becomes harder than it would have been.

On the other hand, some adults who are returning to college or graduate school assume they will find that academic work is too hard for them. They are afraid that they have lost their academic ability, or that they can't become strong enough students. These adults need to develop more confidence that their greater experience, maturity, and motivation will help them maintain their rigorous schedule and excel in their studies.

People of all ages and academic backgrounds have improved the ways they read, write, and study. You can, too.

Part I:
Some Basic Ideas
and Strategies

1

Self-Evaluation

Checklist of factors involved in reading, writing, and studying

Identifying specific areas in which you need to improve is the best first step to meeting your needs. Recognizing your strengths as well as weaknesses in reading, writing, and studying can increase your optimism about the process, which will help you improve more and sooner.

The checklist below can help you evaluate your strengths and weaknesses.

1. In the columns on the right, check the factors that seem to you to be areas of need or concern, either major or minor.

2. In the columns on the left, check the factors that seem to you to be areas of strength.

3. Leave the line blank next to any factor that is neither a strength nor a need or concern for you.

4. Add any additional factors that seem significant to you as strengths or needs or concerns.

Using the checklist

If most of the needs or concerns that you checked have to do with problems in reading, writing, and study skills (the upper part of the checklist), and most of your strengths are attitudes (the lower part), this guidebook is likely to be all that you need in order to read, write, and study more effectively and efficiently.

CHECKLIST

Date of first check _____	Date of recheck _____	Year of last vision test _____

Area of strength	Factors in reading, writing, study	Need or concern	
		Major	Minor
	Comprehending written material		
	Responding critically and creatively		
	Retaining information		
	Taking notes from reading		
	Taking notes from listening		
	Time management		
	Vocabulary		
	Pronouncing unfamiliar words		
	Taking examinations		
	Writing papers		
	Rate of reading		
	Self-image as a reader		
	Self-image as a writer		
	Tension when reading		
	Preparation in previous school(s)		
	Present curriculum		
	Present instruction		
	Support/pressures from home		
	Coping with present environment		
	Attitude toward reading		
	Attitude toward writing		
	Concentration		
	Self-confidence		
	Willpower		
	Motivation		
	Procrastination		
	Certainty/uncertainty about goals		
	Additional factors:		

If you have checked both skills and attitudes as needs or concerns (especially the attitudinal factors of poor concentration and lack of willpower and motivation), you are likely to need more than this guide in order to improve.

You might best avail yourself of some combination of the aids provided by a university reading/writing improvement service or learning resource center. These services are likely to include the following:

1. Interviews to help students evaluate their strengths and needs in reading, writing, and study

2. Reading/writing/study improvement courses

3. Individual tutoring

4. Instructional materials designed to be used independently

5. Workshops on controlling test anxiety

6. Referrals for personal and/or career counseling

7. Referrals for tutoring in oral or written expression

8. Referrals for a vision test.

When you have incorporated many of the procedures recommended in this book into your reading and studying habits, recheck the checklist. Use a different color pen or a different symbol so that you can easily compare your present self-evaluation with your earlier one.

If your re-evaluation indicates that attitudinal factors still contribute to your reading or study problems, consultation with a counseling psychologist is probably desirable. If your re-evaluation indicates that skill factors still contribute to your reading or study problems, consultation with a reading/writing/study specialist at a university learning resource center should be helpful.

If you have strong fears about taking examinations and aren't sure whether you should consult a professional about them, use the following self-evaluation regarding test anxiety, which was developed by Dr. Leonard Miller, associate director and senior psychologist at University of Pennsylvania Counseling and Psychological Services.

Self-evaluation regarding test anxiety*

There are many reasons that account for students not doing well on examinations: being unprepared, feeling ill, missing an important lecture or assignment, being distracted by noise in or around the testing room, and so forth. Some students do not do well on examinations because they become overly tense and test-anxious.

1. *Do you block or freeze when studying for an exam?*

2. *Do you go blank during exams?*

3. *Do you frequently forget information that you previously learned?*

4. *Do you find the words meaningless as you read test questions?*

5. *Do you need to reread test questions in order to comprehend them?*

6. *Do you find yourself plotting ways to escape from a test (sneaking out, feigning illness)?*

7. *Do you—before, during, or after exams—have physical symptoms such as rapid heart rate, excessive perspiration, tense muscles, queasy stomach, nausea?*

8. *Do you have difficulty maintaining concentration while studying or taking exams?*

9. *Do you panic as time runs out during an exam?*

10. *Do you worry about how you are doing on an exam compared to others taking it?*

11. *Do you worry about failing an exam?*

12. *Do you find yourself wishing you were out of school, working – especially just before exams?*

* Copyright © 1979 by Leonard Miller. Reprinted with permission.

13. *Do you panic on a test if you don't know the answer to a question?*

14. *Do you get distracted easily while taking an exam?*

15. *Do you find that you get so tired from worrying about exams that by the time the test comes you almost don't care how well you do?*

If you answered "yes" to many of the questions above, you may have test anxiety. If so, you should seek help as soon as possible from a mental health professional who is trained to help people control their anxiety.

2

Organizing Work
and Budgeting Time

Organizing work and budgeting time are essential to effective
and efficient reading and studying. To take these essential steps,
you will need a calendar/memorandum book. If you don't own
such a book, or at least a calendar with large blocks for each
date, buy one or the other as soon as possible.

Specific suggestions about organizing work and budgeting time
are included with almost every kind of reading, writing, and
studying described in this guide.

Three general recommendations should be helpful at this point:

1. **Keep in mind the useful concepts of "chunking" and
    "clustering."**

    "Chunking," as used in this book, means identifying the
    parts or subgroups of extended materials or tasks, in order
    to accomplish more readily and effectively what you need
    to do. Chunking can help prevent procrastination and
    improve concentration and memory.

    Chunking when you read and study is like chunking when
    you eat. When you eat meat, you chunk by cutting up the
    meat, then you chew and swallow one bite at a time; when
    you eat peas, you cluster peas on your fork, then you chew
    and swallow the group all together.

    Similarly, when you read and study you should chunk and
    cluster: cut up the pieces that are too large for one bite and
    group items too small for one bite. To digest a textbook

chapter, don't read the chapter from beginning to end. Instead, chunk it by sections. (See "Mastering textbook material" and "Studying math and technical subjects" in chapter 6.)

To prepare for an exam, first get an overall view of the total material to be covered, perhaps by making a table of contents for your class notes and reading the chapter summaries of all chapters in a comprehensive book on the subject. Then chunk the material and study one chunk at a time.

······································

When you read and study you should "chunk" and "cluster"; cut up pieces too large for one bite and group items too small for one bite.

When you have to learn many details, like new foreign words or scientific terms, cluster by grouping about five words that are related in some way, then study the words one cluster or group at a time. You can fit these brief study tasks into short periods of time, such as when you are waiting for a train.

You can apply the idea of chunking to many tasks you find difficult to begin or to complete, such as packing for a long trip, organizing stacks of many kinds of material that you've accumulated in a spare room, filing hundreds of articles you've clipped from magazines and newspapers, or planning your sabbatical or retirement.

The notion of chunking is useful for simply noting what you have to do each day. For instance, you can write *call, see,* and *do* at intervals down a memo page and jot down your

notes under the appropriate category. Similarly, on separate
pages, you can write at the top, in order, each of the next
two months and the next three seasons. (I group these
pages in my small loose-leaf memo book behind an alphabetic divider labeled *E* for *eventually*.) Whenever you think
of something you should do within these periods, write it
on the appropriate page. When the time comes to note
what you have to do for each day in the next month or season, retrieve your earlier ideas by consulting your lists for
that month or season.

2. **Estimate time.**

Estimate the time each chunk of your tasks is likely to
require, and estimate the amount of time you have available
each day of the week for such tasks. For courses, assume
that you'll need three study hours for every class hour. As
you look over your plans for a particularly crowded day,
note next to each task the approximate amount of time the
task is likely to take. Add up the time periods you've noted
and consider the result. You are likely to feel amazed and
relieved that the many separate tasks that seemed so bur-
densome will fit into the time you have available, so you
can work more effectively and efficiently – and also look
forward to the recreation you'll have time for, after all.

Sometimes, however, you may find that the tasks do not fit
into the time available or that unexpected responsibilities or
opportunities arise. Some tasks will have to be postponed
until another day. If you note in your memorandum book
when you plan to accomplish the tasks that must be postponed, you are likely to concentrate better on the work at
hand.

In estimating the time you have available for academic or
professional reading/writing/studying, allow for ample and
regular sleep. Sleep is essential to maintain your health,
reduce tension and anxiety, and restore your brain, so that
you can concentrate longer and think and remember better.

3. Safeguard your calendar, reminders, and plans.

Every month or so, photocopy the pages in your pocket calendar and memorandum book on which you have made recent notations. Put the photocopies in a safe place in your home or office, as backups, to avoid being concerned about misplacing or losing the originals.

Many people with various kinds of learning differences or disabilities have considerable difficulty organizing their work and managing their time. When they're motivated to improve, these people are likely to improve much sooner if they get help from a teacher or counseling psychologist with solid professional education and experience in helping students like them.

3

Remembering Effectively

The following information about remembering supports many of the suggestions in this guide.* If, as you read this book, you wonder why a particular suggestion is made, you will probably find the reasons among these principles.

To remember effectively, whether the amount of material is small or large, you need to develop helpful attitudes and procedures.

These are helpful attitudes:

1. **Care about, or be genuinely interested in, remembering the information.**

2. **Give full attention to what is to be remembered.**

3. **Impress the information on your mind clearly and correctly the first time you encounter it.**

4. **Associate what you want to learn with other related information.**

5. **Think, "I *will* remember." (An intent to remember is essential to effective remembering.)**

These are helpful procedures:

1. **Think of details to be learned in terms of a related structure, or create a visually memorable structure for them.**

2. **If there are more than five details, group them in appropriate clusters.**

---

* The information is derived from: Donald A. Norman's *Memory and Attention* (New York: Wiley, 1976), James Weinland's *How to Improve Your Memory* (New York: Harper and Row, 1986), and Barry Gordon's *Memory* (New York: Mastermedia, 1995).

3. **Process the information by using several senses while thinking about the information.**

For example, recite aloud what you can recall from the material you read, and check for accuracy; write briefly what you recall, and check for accuracy; discuss what you are learning with others.

4. **Review the information within twenty-four hours, preferably before sleep.**

5. **Use mnemonics (devices for remembering) that are significantly, rather than artificially, related to the material to be remembered.**

For example, a device for remembering three main elements of good writing is "CUE," which stands for Clarity, Unity, and Emphasis. (See "An example of grouping ideas in significant ways," in chapter 14.)

· ·

Think of details to be learned in terms of a related structure, or create a visually memorable structure for them.

To remember extended reading material, you should also:

Preview	1.	Impress upon your memory the *internal* organization of the new material before reading the material further.
	2.	Connect the information with related *external* information.
Select and chunk	3.	Chunk the material into units that are appropriate to its organization and contain no more than seven items each.
Process deeply	4.	Process the material chunk by chunk (in effect, chew and swallow each chunk before biting off another chunk).
	5.	Write down and discuss with others your ideas about the material you want to remember.

Part II:
Ways to Read, Write, Study, and Take Tests in Various Fields

4

Improving Listening and Note-Taking from Listening

Listening, like reading, should be active; it should involve constant thinking, making connections, and evaluating. Note-taking from listening, like note-taking from reading, should include not only what the speaker or writer said, but also a critical response to what was said or written. In short, you need to make notes as well as take notes.

....

Listening, like reading, should be active. . . . You need to <u>make</u> notes as well as <u>take</u> notes.

Below are comments from students of mine who have tried the methods of taking and making notes that are recommended in this section.

> *"By learning to take good notes the first time around, I've saved a great amount of time by not recopying notes, as well as by the new ways I study the notes."*

> *"Going over my class notes within twenty-four hours... is much quicker than going over them two months later when it's all from the distant past."*

"By using more creative ways to review my notes, I under-stand and remember the material much better. Before... all I would do was read my notes over and then I would forget most of the stuff. I would be frustrated because I didn't remember and I would think that I was stupid. To avoid that, I often didn't bother going over my notes at all until right before the exam and so I had to cram."

1. **Prepare for listening and learning.**

   a) When you know the subject in advance, preview or review related reading in order to recognize and organize the main ideas and terms more easily (that is, increase your background in the subject in a way that makes clear its general organization or structure and some key terms).

   b) To prepare for a seminar, recitation, or meeting in which you are expected to join in the discussion, you will need to do most of the related reading in advance. Previewing is not likely to be sufficient, as it might be for a lecture alone. Note the questions that occur to you while you're reading so that you have them ready when you are listening, discussing, and note-taking.

   c) Use a large loose-leaf notebook for note-taking so that you can rearrange the pages for study purposes, such as comparing, contrasting, and synthesizing the information.

2. **Create notes that will provide a visually memorable impression of the organization of the material.**

   a) Write only on the front side of the loose-leaf page so that your writing will show up clearly (no writing will show through from the other side) and so that you can rearrange the material without having to flip over pages.

   b) Use deep indentations to impress upon your mind the relationship between supporting ideas and organizing ideas. Most sections of this book include paragraphs that are indented, to make the relationship of the points as clear and memorable as possible. Similarly, when you take notes from listening, indent each subordinate idea about an inch, in relation to the main or "organizing" idea that you have noted above it.

··································

Use deep indentations to impress upon your mind the relationship between supporting ideas and organizing ideas.

c) In a class for which note-taking seems especially difficult, leave blank lines at the end of each paragraph or section so that later you can fill in clarifying or supplementary information.

3. **Save time by using appropriate abbreviations and symbols.**

a) For each course or lecture, decide on abbreviations for words that are likely to be used frequently. Note your code on the top of the first page on which you use the abbreviation, or on a page set aside for the purpose. For example:

> p = poetry
>
> compr'n = comprehension
>
> rdg = reading

b) For all courses, learn and use standard (not personal) symbols. Consult the appendix of a large dictionary for standard symbols. For example:

> $\rightarrow$ leads to or results in
>
> $\leftarrow$ results from
>
> $\equiv$ is defined as

$\therefore$ therefore

$\Rightarrow$ implies

$\not\Rightarrow$ does not imply

c) For scientific courses, buy a dictionary specific to the subject, and consult its list of standard abbreviations and symbols in the field.

d) Note: Abbreviations and symbols can save time in writing answers on essay examinations and they are generally acceptable (1) if they are standard, and (2) if, for one or two proper names that will be repeated frequently, you indicate a code on the top of the page (for example, T = Tchaikovsky).

4. **Include brief notes of any of the lecturer's anecdotes or illustrations that impress you as especially effective.**

These can help you remember the information that they illustrate, and they can help you if you need to explain the material to others – days or even years later.

5. **Include in your notes useful comments that you or other students make in discussion during the class or seminar.**

In the margin next to the comment write the name of the person who spoke.

6. **During (and after) listening, note on a separate page your own ideas in response to what you have heard.**

a) Noting your own ideas and questions can prevent your speaking out in class prematurely and can enhance your clarity and fluency in speaking when and if you decide to do so.

b) Your personal notes can be helpful also in guiding your future reading and in providing a source of ideas or questions for research papers and exam answers.

Review your notes within 24 hours.

c) Collecting notes, on separate pages, about your instructors' methods can be valuable during courses and in years to come. Include notes about the instructor's approach to or method of thinking about the subject, and try to apply a similar approach or method. Write down the teaching methods and behavior that you found especially effective or ineffective. Your notes will remind you of methods and behavior you would like to emulate or avoid, if you have an opportunity to be an instructor yourself.

7. **Review your notes within twenty-four hours, preferably within a half hour.**

a) As soon as possible after listening, read over your notes: make corrections where necessary, add clarifying notes on the lines left blank, and note personal comments and questions on a separate page (or on the back of the preceding page).

b) Underline organizing ideas and key terms with a colored pen or pencil (a small ruler can speed up this process).

c) Recite aloud, from memory, the ideas you have reviewed.

— After reviewing each chunk, recite four to seven subpoints that you noted about a single organizing idea.

— At the end, recite the organizing ideas for four to seven chunks.

8. **When taking notes from reading material related to lectures and discussions, insert the page references of your notes from reading into the margins of your notes from listening.**

Or, briefly note the ideas you gained from your reading on the blank back of the notebook page opposite your lecture notes on the same subject.

The learner... *should always recollect and review his lectures, read over some other author or authors upon the same subject, confer about it with his instructor or with his associates, and write down the clearest result of his present thoughts, reasonings, and inquiries, which he may have recourse to hereafter, whether to re-examine them, and to apply them to proper use, or to improve them further to his own advantage.*

Isaac Watts
The Improvement of the Mind
London, 1741

5

Saving Time in Taking Notes from Reading: The A-to-E Method

To save time in taking notes from library books or other material that you should not mark up, imagine that every page is divided into five horizontal sections invisibly labeled A to E, like this.

On a double-column page, the left column can be imagined as labeled *A* to *E*; the right, *a* to *e*.

Using this method, your reading and note-taking for a research paper would go like this:

1. **Write on the reverse side of your bibliographical card the page numbers and parts of pages (that is, A to E) on which you find promising material.**

    For example, notations for your paper on ideas for a new English curriculum might look like this:

    On one side of the card:

    > Whitehead, Alfred North, THE AIMS OF
    > EDUCATION AND OTHER ESSAYS. New York:
    > The Macmillan Co., 1957.

    On the reverse side:

~~2C~~	18C	338DE
3A	21A	35E
6C-E	27DE	38-39A
7A	38B	~~47E~~
13D,E*	10BE	57A
14E	~~31F~~	

2. **After finishing a book (or as many books as you want to read before taking notes on the material), return to the pages that you have indicated on the back of each bibliographical card.**

    Type notes on index cards or make notes on your computer from the material that now seems essential. Cross out the page notations that you decide are not useful after all (see examples above).

3. **As you read, continually reflect upon what you have read and make notes about your ideas and feelings about the material.**

    a) If the book or article belongs to you, put erasable brackets in the margin to mark lines you might want to reread. Put question marks or asterisks in the margin to

---

* The comma means that some material in the middle of DE should not be noted.

refer to fuller comments you write. Write these comments on separate paper, rather than in the margin, to provide for more space, more ease in photocopying if necessary, and longer usefulness and availability. These advantages will be especially evident if the book or article disappears, or if newer editions are released and you want to save your ideas about the earlier ones but not the older editions themselves.

b) For research papers, make notes on separate cards so that you can organize these with your other notes for incorporation in your paper.

c) For supplementary reading, make notes on full-size paper, with page references in the margin, so that you can include these with your notes on the book's content when you review for exams.

d) See chapter 7 for ideas about how you can intensify your reflection about your reading and improve the quality of the notes you take on your reflections.

6

Developing Reading Versatility

Listed below are suggestions for developing a habit of approaching reading in ways appropriate for your purposes and the nature of the material – that is, for developing reading versatility.

To increase your interest, concentration, and speed in reading material for which you have little or no background, develop background on the subject before the reading. You can do this in three main ways: attend a lecture on the subject, preview and selectively read material on a similar subject that is easier for you or has more illustrations, or try to have an appropriate firsthand experience related to the subject.

Reading rapidly for key ideas only

1. **Every day, choose reading material that you want to read but that you are not required to learn, that you find relatively easy, and that looks readable (short lines, clear print).**

2. **Using the material of your choice, practice the following exercises for about fifteen minutes every day:**

   a) Focus on the title of the article. Quickly review what you already know and think or feel about the subject.

   b) Preview expository (nonfiction) material by reading the last paragraphs, headings, and/or first sentence in every few paragraphs – preview any organizational aids that might provide, in effect, a map of the material.

c) Tell yourself what you know about the material as a result of the preview.

d) Turn the title into a question, or think of a question of interest to you that is likely to be answered in the material. (In reading an article entitled "New Hope for the Slow Reader," you might ask yourself, "What is the new hope for the slow reader, and is there hope for me?")

e) To answer your question, read more rapidly than is really comfortable for you. Concentrate on key ideas, not on your eye movements. Your eyes will move faster automatically when you comprehend the content faster.

f) After reading as much as you can in this way (usually after encountering four to seven key ideas), ask yourself what you recall in answer to your question. If you skip this step, you will probably forget what you have read, unless you discuss it with someone that day or have a strong interest in the subject.

g) If you can't remember, you may have gone too fast. Review the material selectively for a fuller answer.

3. **Measure your increasing ability to read *appropriate* material rapidly.**

For example, consider approximately how much more material you are able to read within the 15-minute practice period from week to week. (Avoid wasting time by counting the number of words you've read per minute.)

Books of importance of any kind, and especially complete treatises on any subject, should be first read in a more general and cursory manner, to learn a little what the treatise promises, and what you may expect from the writer's manner and skill.

And for this end I would advise always that the preface be read, and a survey taken of the table of contents, if there be one, before this very first survey of the book. By this means you will not only be better fitted to give the book the first reading, but you will be much assisted in your second perusal of it, which should be done with greater attention and deliberation, and you will learn with more ease and readiness what the author pretends to teach.

Isaac Watts, 1741

Reading expository material for study purposes

Expository material includes books and articles listed in bibliographies, *not* major textbooks that should be mastered, and *not* imaginative literature.

When students are asked to comment on the value of the steps suggested below for reading expository material, they are especially enthusiastic about the time-saving value of previewing. For example:

"'Previewing' is the most exciting word I've learned in years, in that it has saved me untold hours of reading or worrying about articles that I thought I had to read completely but really had little need for or interest in."

"Sometimes I learn all I want or need to learn just by previewing the article."

"Previewing reading material helps me to be more selective in my choices, and I am able to read more material at a faster rate."

"By previewing, I have found that there are many readings that I need not read completely, and there are difficult arti-

cles that I can lay aside, when I am tired or not motivated, to read later – and better."

1. Preview

a) Preview the assignment, including:

— the preface and/or table of contents

— the summary and conclusions (this alone may be sufficient for the preview)

— all headings or the first sentence in each long paragraph (if the summary and conclusions are insufficient).

b) Ask yourself from memory what you have learned from the preview.

c) If you take a long break before you complete the assignment, preview again before continuing where you left off.

2. Question

a) Think about:

— the purposes of the instructor in making the assignment

— the apparent purposes of the author

— your purposes in reading the material.

b) Formulate and note a few questions related to the purposes you've thought about.

3. Read

Read to answer the questions you've formulated.

4. Recite

Pause occasionally to try to answer the questions you've formulated.

5. Write

Take brief notes during reading:

> — by bracketing in the margins and/or by very sparse underlining (if the book is your own)

> — by noting pages and parts of pages (A to E) from which you may want to take written notes eventually (see chapter 5).

6. Review, reflect, write

a) Take more extensive notes after reading, and include ideas of your own in response to the material.

> — For summarizing, write from your page notations, on full-size paper, with sufficient indentations to show the relationships between the organizing ideas and supporting ideas.

> — For research papers, take notes from your page notations on 3x5 index cards.

b) When your reading and note-taking are complete, reread all your notes, think about what you've read, and add more notes on your reflections. (See "Questioning to encourage critical and creative reading" in chapter 7.)

Mnemon, even from his youth to his old age… when he came to the end of a section or chapter, … always shut his book, and recollected all the sentiments or expressions he had remarked, so that he could give a tolerable analysis and abstract of every treatise he had read, just after he had finished it. Thence he became so well furnished with a rich variety of knowledge.

Isaac Watts, 1741

Mastering textbook material

Your old habits for studying textbooks may seem hard to change, but better ways to study can prove so helpful that changing becomes easier than continuing old ways. Here are comments from undergraduates and graduate students who tried the procedures recommended in this section and evaluated them:

> *"When I preview a chapter just before a lecture, I find the lecture easier to understand."*

> *"Previewing helps me get into studying and overcome procrastination."*

> *"The skill of previewing and the idea of getting 'the whole' of the structure before reading helps me integrate the details and retain the information much more effectively."*

> *"I was a meticulous underliner, using a myriad of glorious colors. Now, instead, I outline on one page only and save at least two hours per chapter."*

Try using one or more of the procedures outlined below, depending on how difficult the material is for you and how thoroughly you should know it. The procedures are like a set of tools from which you should select according to your need. You are not likely to need every one of them for every assignment.

Within twenty-four hours before a lecture on the subject:

1. **Preview the chapter.**

    a) Ask yourself, "What do I already know about the subject of the chapter?"

    b) Read a portion of the table of contents to see how this chapter is related to the ones preceding and following it.

    c) Read the summary of the chapter (usually to be found near the end or at the beginning). If the summary seems clear and full, skip items (d) and (e) below.

    d) If the summary seems inadequate, read all the headings

in the chapter and/or the first sentence in every long
paragraph.

e) Study (learn all you can from) pictures, maps, and other
graphic aids.

f) After each step above, ask yourself, "What do I know
about the subject now?" and quickly recite your answer
to yourself. Check back for accuracy.

Attend the lecture (see chapter 4)

Within twenty-four hours after the lecture:

2. **Ask yourself a question, then read each section of the
chapter.**

a) Establish a purpose for reading each section. Either
make up a question to keep in mind as you read the section (this can be the heading restated as a question, like
"What in heaven's name *are* Double Stars?"), or read
one of the problems listed at the end of the chapter (as
in math and chemistry textbooks).

· ·

*Establish a <u>purpose</u> for reading
each section of a chapter. . . .
Read to answer a question or
solve a problem.*

b) Read to answer the question or to solve the problem.
(If the material is very difficult, read the first sentence in
every paragraph of the section before reading the
section fully.)

3. **Recite.**

a) Tell yourself, in your own words and from memory, the

answer to the question you kept in mind as you read (plus anything else you remember from the section), or solve the problem.

b) If you can't remember adequately, skim the section again and recite again.

c) Continually tell yourself, "I *will* remember."

4. **Write.**

a) After reading (and reciting) each section, note the main point (the organizing idea, or perhaps just the heading) of the section.

1) Indent deeply to show the relationship between main ideas and sub-ideas, and to create a visually memorable outline or "map" of the chapter.

2) Keep your notes so brief that they fit easily on one page (or one page for every twenty to twenty-five pages of text); your notes should serve simply as a cue sheet to aid your memory.

3) If the book is your own, underline a few words and bracket the most important lines in the section. Avoid the temptation to highlight line after line of type with a colored marker. Heavy highlighting is actually a procrastination technique; it usually means "This is what I should learn eventually – but not now." Students who overuse highlighting usually think little and remember little about the material they read. They often end up cramming for exams, and they are likely to quickly forget most of the information.

4) Note in the margins of your lecture notes the pages in your text that are on the same subject.

b) On another sheet of paper, write down any questions that come to your mind about the material, or any new insights you may have on this or other related subjects. Keep in mind: previewing and making a one-page outline will provide you with a map of the chapter's subject. Like any map, it might contain errors. Also, other maps of the same subject may be needed to provide different kinds of information and a different perspective.

5. Review and reflect.

When you have completed the chapter (and the one-page outline), reread the outline, underline the main points, and recite as much as you can from memory. Again, reflect and add any new ideas to the sheet of paper that is separate from the outline. Noting your ideas and questions can help you in your further reading, as well as in your class discussions.

To summarize, here is the rack of tools* with which to master a textbook chapter. To remember all the steps, use the formula "PQ6R" – Preview, Question, Read, Recite, Write, Review, Reflect, Review.

Tools		Check if used
Preview	Survey the whole chapter, and recite from memory what you have learned so far.	
Question	Set a purpose: formulate a question or read one of the problems listed.	
For each chapter section:		
Read	Read one section (chunk) to answer the question or to solve the problem. Bracket main ideas in the margin.	
Recite	Recite your answer to the question, or solve the problem.	
Write	Write a line or two toward forming a one-page outline of the whole chapter.	
After finishing the chapter:		
Review	Review the completed one-page outline. Recite it from memory.	
Reflect	Reflect critically and creatively. Write brief notes about your reflections and questions on a page separate from the one-page outline.	
Review	Review the one-page outline again within twenty-four hours.	

* Most of these steps are derived from the procedure described by Francis P. Robinson in his book *Effective Study*, rev. ed. (New York: Harper and Row, 1961).

Studying math and technical subjects

Studying mathematics and technical subjects such as engineering primarily involves solving problems. How can you learn more in less time in these subjects?

1. **Find and impress upon your memory a structured overview of the material that you have to learn.**

    a) Before starting work on the first problems in a course, preview and read the introductory or summary chapter of the textbook.

    b) Before reading each subsequent chapter, study the organizational aids in the chapter – the summary, the headings, and the graphic material that can give you a visually memorable "map" of the whole chapter.

2. **Follow the chronology recommended in the previous section, "Mastering textbook material":**

    Preview the chapter within 24 hours before the class on the same subject, thus impressing on your mind a structure and terminology that will help you take good lecture notes; attend the lecture; then, within twenty-four hours, while the lecture is fresh in your mind, review your lecture notes and study the chapter in the way described below.

3. **Study the chapter in appropriate chunks – usually one problem per chunk.**

    a) Study math and technical subjects as actively as possible, primarily by solving problems and explaining your solutions to someone else (or aloud to yourself, at least). Merely being able to understand a sample problem shows promise but is inadequate evidence of your understanding and is too passive for insuring mastery.

    Studying a chapter in a math or engineering textbook would go like this:

    1) Read the first problem, or the first assigned problem, at the end of the section or chapter.

2) Read the explanatory section until you think you can work the problem.

3) Work the problem.

4) Proceed similarly through the rest of the chapter; read the next assigned problem, read the explanatory section of the text, and work the problem – so that when you have finished the chapter you have also finished the assigned problems.

5) In engineering texts, work at least a few of the many examples of each kind of problem, even if you can easily follow the sample problem and solution given. This can help you feel more confident that you have fully mastered each kind of problem.

A distinction between engineering textbooks and physics textbooks is that most engineering texts emphasize using only one essential method to solve a variety of problems, whereas many physics textbooks emphasize using a variety of methods to solve one problem in order to illuminate fully the physical principles involved.

b) Studying a chapter in a textbook on organic chemistry or physics would be similar, but with some exceptions:

1) Read the sample problem at the end of one section, read the section, then work the sample problem. Wait until you have finished studying all the sections in the chapter before you read and work the problems at the end of the chapter.

This method is preferable in these two sciences because part of understanding them is recognizing which concept applies in a given problem, as well as recognizing how a single concept works in different contexts.

2) Of the thirty to fifty problems at the end of the chapter, do two or three of each type (about ten

altogether), unless more are assigned. (See "Solving problems in physics," below.)

4. **Be very organized in laying out the problems you work.**

   a) Follow the layout shown in the text's samples.

   b) Draw figures and visualize the problem before you work it mathematically. Visualizing the problem is essential to solving it – it helps you understand the problem better, and enables you to check one type of reasoning against another. On examinations, as well as in regular assignments, solve the problems geometrically as well as mathematically.

· ·

Draw figures and visualize the problem before you work it mathematically.

5. **Work with a small group of other students on your homework problems, if your instructor approves.**

   This can give you a vital opportunity to actively use your new technical terms as you discuss how you arrived at your answers to the problems.

You should study in these ways for three main reasons:

   1. The more background you have about a subject—background that is appropriately structured—the more readily you can learn, remember, and apply new information about the subject.

   2. To remember extended material, you need to learn one piece at a time, keeping in mind the pattern into which each piece fits. The best way to learn each piece is to use or apply it in an appropriately structured way.

3. Discussing problems with other students can help you learn better in many ways, especially because it involves using several senses while thinking about the subject. It can help you clarify your thinking and increase your motivation to learn and remember.

You will need to cope with elements of the course in addition to the textbook. In math and technical courses, instructors may not always follow the book exactly; in class, they may spend more time on some areas, leave out other areas, and even add areas not included in the book. Usually, instructors assign homework from the problems at the back of the book – but their exams may include problems that are different from those in the book. Ask your instructor for copies of old exams, or see if they are on file in a learning center. Using the old exams, practice applying what you have learned from class and the homework on problems similar to those that you will face on your next exam.

Solving problems in physics

Dr. Roger Walmsley, Professor of Physics at the University of Pennsylvania for many years, shared with me the suggestions he offers his students about solving physics problems. With his generous permission, I'm passing along some of his suggestions:

Keep in mind there are various ways to solve physics problems, not just one way. Some people or books might claim to offer the one "correct" way, but many physics professors will tell you that a "correct" way is simply an example of one of the different but equivalent ways to solve physics problems. If you exercise your imagination and intellect, you can develop your own style of problem-solving; however, you will have to be able to explain your way and defend it.

After following the three basic steps for studying physics that are described in the preceding section, try these additional steps:

1. **Reread the first problem at the end of the chapter and ask yourself, "What section or sections in the chapter relate to this problem?"**

2. **Visualize the situation described in the problem.**

   What does it look like? What are the spatial relationships of the parts, and how do the objects move? Describe to yourself—even write down—what you visualize.

3. **Think about the principles that apply to the situation in the problem.**

   With these principles in mind, devise a coherent strategy for answering each question in the problem. For each equation, ask yourself, "What do I have to know in order to arrive at the answer to this question?"

4. **If the problem is very complex, break it into sections and handle one section at a time.**

   Then, assemble the whole answer to the complex problem, using the relationships of the sections to one another.

5. **If you get stuck, reread the relevant parts of the text, and look at the examples and other problems that involve the same concepts.**

   If you're still stuck, put the problem aside for awhile.

6. **When you come back fresh to the problem, you're likely to think of a strategy for solving it.**

Reread the questions and be sure that your strategy leads to an answer to the actual questions asked. Dr. Walmsley emphasizes, "Resist the temptation to misconstrue the questions in a way that makes them amenable to the strategy you conceived."

Reading fiction or poetry for full effect and meaning

The recommendations below can help you think more critically about literature and also help you find more personal value in reading it. A professor's questions may call attention primarily to the artistic elements of the literature, such as the plot, characters, and setting of a novel; another's may call attention primarily to the author; yet another's to the world that influenced the literature or is reflected in it, and so on. You are likely to be more interested and successful in thinking about literature from different points of view if you first note your personal response to it, then note your critical or interpretive response to it, and finally reconsider your personal response.

The personal values for which you read literature may include entertainment, beauty, self-understanding, understanding others, and inspiration to change society. While all of these values can be derived from most good literature, the values of a particular literary piece may be different for each reader. This is because readers naturally bring different experiences, interests, and needs to the same piece, and thus respond in different ways emotionally, imaginatively, and intellectually.

1. **Consider—and note in writing—during and after reading fiction or poetry:**

   a) the effect of the fiction or poetry on you – emotionally, imaginatively, and intuitively, as well as intellectually.

   b) the scenes, lines, phrases, and images that impressed you most.

·······························

Note the effect that the fiction or poetry has on you.

2. **Tentatively and briefly, try to answer the following questions (knowing that you will answer them again when you have studied the work more thoroughly):**

   a) Considering the novel, short story, or poem as a whole, what do you think it means? In brief, what seem to be its themes? State the themes carefully, avoiding statements that are too narrow or too broad.

   b) What view of life, or attitude toward life, does the novel, story, or poem reveal? What is your reaction to this view or attitude?

c) What is the value of the novel, story, or poem to you personally? Have you found it entertaining? Have you found beauty in it? Has it helped you understand yourself or others? How has the experience of reading it changed you – your attitudes, your feelings, your thinking?

d) What experiences have you had, and what tendencies do you have as a reader, that might be affecting your response?

e) What might be the value of this work of art to others? Could it help change society?

3. If you wish or need to understand the fiction or poetry more fully, analyze it in detail.

Consider how each element of the work contributes to its total effect and meaning. A work of art is organic, like a tree or a person; in analyzing it, you need to consider how each element that composes it relates to other elements and to the whole. For detailed questions that might help you analyze fiction, see item 5, below. For help taking notes to support your analysis, use the time-saving ABCDE method described in chapter 5. For notes that might help you ana-

lyze poetry, see "Taking notes from poetry..." in chapter 7.
(After analyzing the novel, story, or poem in detail, consider
again items 1 and 2, above.)

4. **Consult one of the following sources on the subject:**

Barnet, Sylvan. *A Short Guide to Writing About Literature,*
7th ed. New York: Watson–Guptill, 1995.

Boynton, Robert W., and Maynard Mack. *Introduction to
the Poem,* 3rd ed. Portsmouth, NH: Boynton/Cook, 1985.

Scholes, Robert, et al. *Elements of Literature: Fiction,
Poetry, Drama, Essay, Film,* 3rd ed. New York: Oxford
University Press, 1991.

5. **In analyzing a work of fiction, consider the following
elements:**

a) Point of view

   1) Is the story told by the author, who knows all? Or
      through one of the characters? Or through several
      of the characters?

   2) Does the narrator seem to be reliable and truthful?
      If not, why not?

   3) What does the point of view contribute to the total
      meaning of the novel?

b) Plot

   1) What is the scope of the novel in time?

   2) What are the main scenes?

   3) Does the action seem to develop because of the
      nature of the characters? Or through societal
      forces? Or through fate?

   4) What is the shape of the story line? Is it a journey
      or quest? A fall or rise in morals or in fortune? A
      meeting or marriage? A growing-up through expe-
      rience? An interweaving of story lines?

  5) Does the plot have an underlying pattern?

  6) What does the plot contribute to the total meaning of the novel?

c) Characters

  1) Are the characters "flat"? (Can they be described fully in a few words? Do they change very little in the novel?) Or are they "round"? (Are many of their qualities revealed? Do they develop during the novel?)

  2) Which characters are most memorable to you? Why?

  3) How are the characters revealed? By what they say and do? By what the narrator says and thinks? By what other characters say? By what the author says directly to the reader?

  4) Do any of the characters contrast with one another in significant ways?

  5) What do the characters contribute to the total meaning of the novel?

d) Setting

  1) What is the scope of the novel in space or setting?

  2) Does the setting seem important to the characters? To the plot?

  3) What does the setting contribute to the total meaning of the novel?

e) Language or diction

  1) Is the novel composed largely of conversation? Does the conversation seem true to life?

  2) Is the novel simply a reporting of events?

  3) Is the novel written with poetic imagery? What are the central images or metaphors?

      4) What is the nature of the diction (the selection of words)? Is it formal? Informal? Colloquial? Slang? Does it change during the course of the novel?

      5) What does the language or diction contribute to the total meaning of the novel?

   f) Tone (a quality of style that reveals or creates attitude, as in "tone of voice")

      1) Is the tone of the novel humorous? Serious? Sarcastic? Grim? Lofty? Conversational? How can you tell?

      2) What does the tone of the novel contribute to its total meaning?

   g) Title

      1) How does the title relate to, or clarify, the overall meaning of the novel?

6. Which of the elements of the novel seem to be the most important?

7. Return to items 1 and 2 in this section, and elaborate on your original responses to the novel.

8. To enhance your appreciation of fiction or poetry, listen to recordings of it that may be available in a bookstore, music store, library, or through mail order.

For more recommendations on reading literature, see "Taking notes from poetry" in chapter 7.

Comments on speed reading

Reading rate is a mental tendency that is seldom improved permanently by external pressure of any kind. Machines and other external devices (for example, a moving hand) designed to increase reading speed are not clearly better than other methods, and they have the major disadvantage that when readers who use external devices read without them, they soon tend to return to their former rate of reading. In contrast, the exercises recommended in "Reading rapidly for key ideas only," at the beginning of this section, do not involve external pressure. They are likely to continually help any reader who feels motivated to do regular exercises that can become good habits.

The disadvantages of speed reading include the following:

1. The pressure to read faster tends to increase the anxiety of students who are already anxious about their reading assignments. As anxiety increases, comprehension usually decreases.

2. Most readers cannot concentrate on their eye movements and on the content of what they are reading at the same time. Therefore, concentration on faster, smoother eye movements usually results in reduced concentration on the content of the material.

3. Speed reading does not insure clear and accurate initial learning, and therefore often creates the time-consuming problem of unlearning and relearning.

Improvement in reading speed as well as comprehension is likely to be greater and more lasting if readers try to improve their central processes (perception, comprehension, assimilation) rather than their peripheral processes (eye movements, as described in Miles Tinker's book, listed below).

Subvocalization, or saying each word silently during reading, can help some readers comprehend or better appreciate what they read. While subvocalization was once considered a crutch to be avoided, it is now recognized as a natural way for some readers to cope with material they find difficult. When readers have more background, confidence, and interest in their reading material, they usually find that they no longer subvocalize, except to appreciate more fully a passage of particularly good writing.

Reading versatility is far more desirable than reading speed. Reading versatility means the ability to adapt reading approach (including rate) to the nature of the reading material and the purpose for which one is reading it. Improvement in reading versatility usually comes with increased background in the subjects at hand, and with increased attention to setting purposes before beginning to read any material.

· ·

Reading versatility is far more desirable than reading speed.

For further information on speed reading, consult the following:

Tinker, Miles, A. "Role of Eye Movements in Improving Reading," in *Bases for Effective Reading*. Minneapolis: University of Minnesota Press, 1965.

Whimbey, Arthur, and Jack Lochhead. "Six Myths about Reading," in *Problem Solving and Comprehension*, 5th ed. Hillsdale, NJ: L. Erlbaum Assocs., 1991.

Clear and distinct apprehension of the things which we commit to memory is necessary in order to make them stick and dwell there.... If we would treasure up the ideas of things, notions, propositions, arguments and sciences, these should be recommended also to our memory by clear and distinct perception of them. Faint glimmering and confused ideas will vanish like images in twilight.

Isaac Watts, 1741

7

Improving Thinking—and Note-Taking from Thinking—about the Material You Read

Adapting to reading and note-taking in an unfamiliar genre or discipline

A major problem when reading and note-taking in a relatively unfamiliar genre or discipline is deciding what to look for and note as significant. How should you read and take notes from poetry assigned in one of your first literature courses? From legal cases in one of your first law courses? From material assigned in a higher-level history or physiology course when you haven't had an introductory course in these disciplines? Before considering some specific answers to these questions, consider the following general points:

1. **Mere reading, or reading and making marks on the page, is not an appropriate method of reading to learn.**

   To follow many of the principles and procedures of remembering (listed in chapter 3), reading to learn should include making notes of your critical and creative thoughts as they occur to you, and taking notes from the content of the material only when you are fairly sure of what is most significant (as described in chapter 5).

2. **If you encounter a word, phrase, sentence, or paragraph you don't understand, pencil a question mark in the margin of the book, and keep reading.**

    When you've come to the end of the material and you return to the question marks, you're likely to have enough perspective and information to comprehend the questioned material more quickly than if you had puzzled over it during the first encounter.

3. **Don't be surprised or concerned if your reading in a new genre or discipline is much slower and more laborious than it is in more familiar material.**

    As your familiarity with the new field increases, your comprehension is likely to be quicker and greater. Moreover, freeing yourself of anxiety about being a "slow reader" or "poor reader" will help raise your comprehension; usually, the higher one's anxiety, the lower one's comprehension.

4. **Above all, find out from authorities in the genre or discipline unfamiliar to you what basic questions or structures might guide your initial reading and note-taking.**

    One authority could be a professor in the discipline, who might offer guidance in a class or conference. You can also analyze lectures to find questions that can guide your reading. Another authority could be a basic current text in the field, or a practitioner or expert beyond the classroom.

5. **By starting with a basic current text, you are likely to increase your background in the subject enough so that you can read more advanced materials with greater ease.**

    You can read the basic text selectively; the methodology section and the summary chapter, or individual chapter summaries, may be sufficient for the purpose of guiding further reading.

·······························

Find out... what basic questions or structures might guide your initial reading.

For comprehensive recommendations about reading and writing in an unfamiliar discipline or genre, consult a handbook written by an authority in the discipline or genre – for example, *Handbook for Research in American History*, 2nd rev. ed. by Francis Paul Purcha (Lincoln: University of Nebraska Press, 1994), for history, or *Psychological Research: An Introduction*, by Arthur J. Bachrach (New York: Random House, 1981), for psychology.

As in all reading and listening, maintain a critical attitude in finding and following a basic structure or questions; that is, be aware that another authority may disagree with the one you've consulted, and that you can bring, from your own knowledge and experience, ideas for expanding or modifying the structure or questions you find.

In the beginning of your application to any new subject, "be not too uneasy under present difficulties that occur, nor too importunate and impatient for answers and solutions to any questions that arise." Perhaps a little more study, a little further acquaintance with the subject, a little time and experience will solve those difficulties, untie the knot, and make your doubts vanish....

Isaac Watts, 1741

Taking notes from textbooks or articles in the biological or physical sciences

In the biological and physical sciences, authorities generally agree on methodology. Therefore, almost any authoritative text designed to be an introduction to the science would be appropriate as a source of a structure or questions to guide initial reading. However, before taking an advanced course in science, a student new to the field will be able to learn more in less time by selectively reading not only an introductory text to the science, but also introductory material regarding the specific area that is the subject of the course.

To study scientific material, follow the suggestions recommended in "Mastering textbook material," in chapter 6. To aid you in "reflecting," see "Questioning to encourage..." in chapter 7, and answer the questions that seem most appropriate for your purposes and for the material. For recommendations about studying physics and chemistry, see "Studying math and technical subjects" in chapter 6.

Taking notes from history books or articles

In history, as in many other disciplines, there are controversies among authorities that should affect critical reading in the field. One of the major controversies among historians today is about whether primary attention should be given to studying the ruling people at the top of society, or the common people at the bottom; that is, historians disagree about whether to study history "from the top down or the bottom up." The old history is from "above"; the New History (so capitalized) is from "below."

A more long-standing controversy, which is still current among historians, is about methodology. The controversy centers on a difference of opinion among historians about whether history should be classified as one of the humanities or as one of the social sciences. Historians who classify history as one of the humanities tend to regard narrative as the primary method of writing history; those who classify history as a social science tend to regard analysis as the primary method. Students for whom history is an unfamiliar discipline should keep this difference of opinion in mind as they read history, and perhaps modify the structure or questions that they gain from any one authority to guide their initial reading.

To illustrate, when I asked a history professor to recommend an authoritative book that might guide an initial reading of history, I was directed to *Doing History* by J. H. Hexter (Indiana University Press, 1971). When I consulted two more historians for additional ideas to include in this section, I learned that Dr. Hexter's view represents one side of a controversy among historians regarding the relative value of analysis, statistical evidence, and the social sciences. Therefore, in using my notes from *Doing History* as a guide in reading history (in this case, *The Emergence of the American University* by Lawrence R. Veysey [Chicago: University of Chicago Press, 1965]), I gave more weight to analysis, statistical evidence, and the social sciences than Hexter implies is necessary.

Following are my notes from *Doing History*, a description of the process by which I took notes from one section of *The Emergence of the American University*, and the notes themselves.

A sample of my notes from reading

for J. H. Hexter, *Doing History*. Bloomington: Indiana University Press, 1971.

*Page
ref.*

15   Definition of "historiography" ("doing history"): "The craft of writing history and/or the yield of such writing considered in its rhetorical aspect" (Hexter)

154   — as a branch of intellectual history: "the history of the ideas of historians about the past"

15   — as a subbranch of the sociology of knowledge: "the history of history writing"

44 Thesis: "The communication and therefore the advancement of historical knowledge is inseparable from the rhetoric of history"; in other words, historians convey knowledge of the past at once by what they write and by the way they write.

51 A. How (and how well) has this historian "done" history? (Only "provisional judgments" are possible, even with knowledge of the historical record.)

    1. Does the historian communicate what-happened-and-how by historical narrative, historical analysis, or both, organically integrated?

27   a. Narrative (telling a story or stories) is "the principle of coherence traditionally and still most generally employed" by historians.

        b. Analysis requires formulation of a rough hypothesis "for which the surviving records hold forth some hope of verification."

    2. How "slight or abundant" is the historical evidence, how "adequate or inadequate" the historical proof?

142   a. Does the evidence include quantification, statistical foundations? (e.g., "one-fortieth of the population" instead of "a tiny fraction"?)

    3. To what extent does the historian use material from the social sciences?

    4. To what extent is this history comparative, as opposed to nationalistic or ethnocentric?

    5. To what extent is the language denotative, to what extent connotative?

        a. Denotative language of historiography is like that of the natural sciences; it may be desirable and necessary to make accounts more complete, exact.

Major difference between use of denotative
language in history and in natural sciences:
"to convey historical reality... with maximum
impact... may require a historian to subordinate completeness, explicitness, and exactness
to other considerations."

43   b. Connotative ("evocative and even metaphori-
cal") language of historiography is "nearer
to the language of the fictive arts"; it may be
desirable and even necessary," in order
to bring the reader "into confrontation with
events long past and men long dead,"
to make accounts "forceful, vivid, lively."

47   Major difference between use of connotative
language in history and in fictive arts: the
"overriding commitment of historians to
fidelity to the surviving records of the past."

25   B. What understanding of the past ("historical reality")
does the historian communicate to me through his
writing?

— what "movement and tempo of events"

— what "motives and actions of men"

— what "impact on the course of events of an accident,
a catastrophe, or a bit of luck..."?

Description of my note-taking process

for *The Emergence of the American University,* by Lawrence
R. Veysey

1. I conjectured that the typical assignment in an advanced history course would involve reading from an extensive bibliography
(rather than mastering one or two textbooks), that most of the
books in the bibliography would be on reserve in the library and
therefore could not be marked, and that notes would have to be
more detailed in order to have sufficient material for review.

2. I read the table of contents to discover the scope of the book, and to locate the pages where the thesis of the book would probably be stated.

3. I looked for a statement of the thesis and elaboration of it in the first and last paragraphs of the preface and the conclusion; when I found what I was looking for (in the first sentences of the opening paragraphs of these sections), I noted the pages and parts of pages from which I would probably want to take notes.

4. Returning to the pages and parts of pages I had noted, I took notes on the thesis, quoting directly for the most part (using quotation marks), because the field is relatively new to me and I did not feel certain yet of paraphrasing accurately and quickly.

5. Looking up from my notes, I recited the thesis to myself in order to impress it more deeply upon my memory, which would help me comprehend more quickly as I read on.

6. I returned to the table of contents to note the main headings that indicate the scope of the book in relation to the thesis.

7. I decided which section of the book interested me most and was therefore the best place to start reading, because it would help me "get into" the book – connect the material directly with my previous knowledge and interests and so increase my attention and comprehension as I read on.

8. I previewed and then read the section of particular interest to me, "The academic standards of the new age," in the chapter entitled "The Tendency to Blend and Reconcile," noting pages and parts of pages from which I might want to take notes.

9. Following the questions suggested to me by Hexter's *Doing History,* modified by what I had learned from other historians, I made notes of my critical response to the section.

10. I took notes on the content of the section. If I were to read the whole book, I would follow steps 8 and 9, then check out the book from the reserve room (overnight or three-day checkout is all that is usually permitted) and type or word-process notes from the content, using my notations of pages and parts of pages.

Note: If I were responsible for mastering the material, I would follow the steps suggested for mastering textbook material in chapter 6, to the extent that they seemed necessary.

My notes on the thesis and scope

of *The Emergence of the American University*

*Page
ref.*

439 *Thesis*

> In America, "the idea of the university ... underwent a process ... of assimilation to the New World environment, accompanied by a profound internal tension and a mingled sense of gain and loss."

vii "The most striking thing about the American university in its formative period is the diversity of mind shown by the men who spurred its development."

viii "The two most important types of academic conflict in the late nineteenth century were over the basic purpose of the new university and over the kind and degree of control to be exerted by the institution's leadership."

> *Scope*
>
> Part 1:
>
> Rival Conceptions of the Higher Learning, 1865–1910
>
> 1. Discipline and Piety
> 2. Utility
> 3. Research
> 4. Liberal Culture
>
> A Season of Reassessment, 1908–1910
>
> Part 2:
>
> The Price of Structure, 1890–1910
>
> 5. The Pattern of the New University (including)

     a. The Gulf between Students and Faculty

     b. The Rise of Administration

   6. The Tendency to Blend and Reconcile

     a. The Growing Merger of Ideals

     b. Business Models for Educational Enterprise

     c. The Academic Standards of the New Age

     d. Varieties of the "New" Administrator

   7. The Problem of the Unreconciled

Conclusion: The University as an American Institution

My notes from one section

of *The Emergence of the American University,* Part 2, 6.c.*

A.   The Academic Standards of the New Age

   1. Increasing emphasis on quantification (objected to by some), e.g., Eliot (Harvard): "Quality being secured, the larger the better."

   2. "Concern for quantitative success tended to inhibit quality"

     a) Administration standards low in new universities (Cornell, Stanford) to insure numbers

     b) Larger faculty-student radio made control of academic standards difficult

   3. Conflicting evidence re expectations of academic performance

     a) Requirements grew somewhat harder, 1865–1910

       1) More students required to repeat courses

       2) Honors programs instituted

     b) But standards of work very low compared to mid-

---

* Abbreviations are not included here, in order to make the notes more readable; had I abbreviated, I would have used a code like this: acad.stds = academic standards; fac. = faculty; st. = students; tchg = teaching; u. = undergraduates.

20th century; e.g., some Harvard students received A's for courses never attended, and only 3 hours of tutoring

4. Improvement of quality difficult because educators disagreed about:

   a) How "serious" undergraduate works should be

   c) "Substantive meaning of seriousness," e.g., scientific vs. humanistic professors; accuracy of footnotes vs. "verbal flair and moral dedication."

My comments

on "The Academic Standards of the New Age"

A. Of particular interest and value to me:

   1. The perspective this section gives me on

      a) college admissions problems, past and present (#1 and #2)

      b) past and present need for student services (e.g., learning centers) to help students study more effectively (#3)

      c) current controversy among historians (#4).

B. How Veysey has "done history" here:

   1. Historical analysis; no narrative in this section

      a) Subthesis statements supported by extensive evidence (nonstatistical), with many footnotes to indicate direct sources, additional sources, or additional details.

      b) Example: "The standard of work at leading institutions, despite the upturn of the years after 1905, remained extraordinarily low by the canons of the mid-twentieth century.... At Yale in 1903 seniors required only an hour or less per day to prepare for all their classes." (Footnote cites three sources of this and of similar information) p. 357

    2. Language almost entirely denotative (as illustrated in quotation above).

C. Sense of the past conveyed:

    1. From this section, a sense of the past is largely the result of:

        a) cumulative effect of abundant evidence solidly organized in support of points made

        b) naming rather than narrating of "movement of events," "motives and actions of men"

        c) background that most readers are likely to bring to the book (familiarity with at least one American university).

Taking notes from poetry in a first course in literature

To improve your reading of and note-taking from poetry, find a basic text on literature in general or on poetry in particular by looking through the books required for introductory courses in literature or poetry. You're likely to learn more readily from introductory books that are clearly organized and relatively free of jargon. Examples of such books are: *A Short Guide to Writing about Literature,* by Sylvan Barnet (6th ed., New York: Harper Collins, 1991) and *Introduction to the Poem,* by Robert W. Boynton and Maynard Mack (3rd ed., Portsmouth, NH: Boynton/Cook, 1985).

Your notes from *Introduction to the Poem,* to guide your reading of poems, would probably look something like this:

1. **Who is the speaker?**

2. **Who is the audience?**

3. **What is the tone (of voice) in which the speaker addresses the audience?**

4. **What is the subject? The theme? The meaning?**

5. **How does the pattern of rhythm and sound contribute to the effect and meaning of the poem?**

6. **What "devices of compression" are apparent?**

    a) understatement

    b) irony

    c) paradox

    d) comparison by means of simile, metaphor, juxtaposition.

7. **How do these devices contribute to the effect and meaning of the poem?**

Your notes on your analysis of a specific poem could follow the structure of the questions above. Consider your notes tentative until after you have reread the poem many times, to find evidence to support each of your statements – especially those about theme and meaning. The authors of *Introduction to the Poem* and authors of other introductory texts on literature probably would agree that *before* analyzing a poem in detail, you should consider and note the impact of the poem upon you, and that *after* analyzing a poem, you should consider and note the value of the poem for you personally. Questions to guide these initial and final responses might be:

1. **What is the total effect of the poem upon you – emotionally, imaginatively, intuitively, sensually, intellectually?**

2. **What is the value of the poem for you personally?**

    How has the experience of reading the poem changed you – your attitudes, your feelings, your thinking?

3. **What experiences have you had, and what tendencies do you have as a reader, that might be affecting your response?**

Once you have developed a clear understanding of some of the ways that poems can convey meaning and affect the reader, you will be able to read and take notes from poems more spontaneously, without direct reference to structures such as the one derived from *Introduction to the Poem*.

Here is an example of notes taken on a poem, following the structure provided by *Introduction to the Poem:*

Art

Herman Melville

In placid hours well-pleased we dream
Of many a brave unbodied scheme.
But form to lend, pulsed life create,
What unlike things must meet and mate;
A flame to melt—a wind to freeze;
Sad patience—joyous energies;
Humility—yet pride and scorn;
Instinct and study; love and hate;
Audacity—reverence. These must mate,
And fuse with Jacob's mystic heart,
To wrestle with the angel—Art.

1. **Immediate total effect:**

   Sense of complexity of art (poetry) and all that contributes to its creation – forces both within and beyond the artist (poet).

2. **Elements (and their evidence in the poem):**

   a) Dramatic situation: Artist (poet) at once contemplating the act of creating art and engaging in that act. (Evidence: Literal and figurative meaning of the words themselves – and their embodiment in a poem.)

   b) Speaker: A dreamer and artist, by implication the creator of this poem on the subject of creating poetry.

   c) Audience: Other dreamers. (Evidence: The grammatical subject and verb of the first two lines are "we dream.")

   d) Tone: 1) Heightening awe. (Evidence: The exclamatory fourth line; quickening alternation of various "unlike things" that must mate, from "a flame to melt – a wind to freeze" to "audacity – reverence"; the culminating reference to a mystical story in the Bible.)

2) "Audacious" effort. (Evidence: Quickening alternation of "unlike things" that must mate and "fuse with Jacob's mystic heart,/To wrestle with the angel – Art.")

e) Rhythm and meter: First five lines are roughly iambic (weak, strong, weak, strong, etc.); the next four lines are dominated by speech rhythms; the last two lines return to the iambic. These contrasts support the contrasts indicated by the words: mere dreaming versus the active meeting and mating of "unlike things"; then the fusing "with Jacob's mystic heart,/to wrestle with the angel – Art."

f) Other sounds: The balance created by the shifts in rhythm (noted above) is strengthened by a roughly similar balance in final rhymes: in the first six lines, every two adjacent lines rhyme; the seventh line is unrhymed; in the last four lines every two adjacent lines rhyme; and lines 3 and 4, 8 and 9 have matching rhymes. The "mating" of the rhymes matches the mating described by the words.

3. Devices of compression

a) Irony: "What unlike things must meet and mate" for the creation of art – and how "brave" and not so brave is the "unbodied scheme" we dream "in placid hours."

b) Paradox: The creation of art requires both an act of love (meeting and mating of "unlike things" within the artist) and an act of conflict (fusing "with Jacob's mystic heart,/To wrestle with the angel – Art").

c) Main metaphors: 1) creation of art :: (is analogous to) the act of love by which a child is created (lines 3 and 4); 2) work of art :: child, offspring; 3) muse of art :: messengers of God, the angel who wrestled with Jacob; 4) the artist (poet) :: Jacob.

d) Juxtaposition: Juxtaposed pairs of unlike things suggest the infinite complexity and balance of opposites within human beings and within their creations.

4. **Subject:**

The creation of art (poetry). (Evidence: The title and the literal and figurative meaning of the words of the poem.)

5. **Theme:**

The complex nature of the creative act, requiring all the human faculties and also involvement of and with the divine.

6. **Meaning:**

Beyond the theme, the poem suggests that the effect upon the artist of creating art is in part similar to the effect upon Jacob of his wrestling with the angel – transformation into a better person.

7. **Value for me personally:**

Effect of the poem is the re-creation of the awe of the poet for the creative act and—through my effort to wrestle with the poem—the realization that reading a poem, like writing one, can be a creative act and so can transform me into a better person. Proof of the truth of the lines by W. H. Auden:

> *A poem—a tall story;*
> *But every good one*
> *Makes us want to know.*

(Want to know, for instance, the story of Jacob and the angel in Genesis 27–33.)

As you read and reread poetry for academic assignments, note any idea or thesis that you could develop as a basis for a paper or an exam answer. The basic structure of your paper or exam answer could be this: tell the context of the poem, then present your idea or thesis and support it by discussing each element in the poem as it relates to the whole design.

Taking notes from legal cases in a first course in law

If you are unaccustomed to reading legal cases (judicial opinions), you could talk with a practicing attorney to learn appropriate procedures and questions that can guide your reading and note-taking in this field until you have personal or professional purposes to guide your reading.

A practicing attorney would be likely to recommend procedures and questions similar to those that follow, because they are useful in the practice of law, as well as for law-school coursework:

1. **Examine the preface and table of contents of your casebook.**

   Preview to see the context of the case you are assigned (that is, the area of the law that the case illustrates).

2. **Gain an overall view of the case.**

   In an official report, a headnote is usually provided for overview, with one brief paragraph for each point in the judicial opinion. (Don't depend on headnotes for accuracy, however.) In a law-school casebook, which does not have headnotes, you can usually get an overview by reading the concluding paragraph of the case, and then reading, from the beginning, the first sentence of each short and medium paragraph, and the first and last sentence of every long paragraph.

3. **Read the entire case, chunking the material and taking notes.**

   Take notes after reading each chunk, according to the following structure:

   a) Facts
      What are the facts of the case? What happened between the parties? Note the facts very briefly.

   b) Nature of the action and procedural status

      1) What is the nature of the action? How did the case get to court? Three examples of the many possibili-

ties here are "A sued B for damages," "A was prosecuted by the state for the crime of ____," or "A sued B for injunctive relief."

2) What is the procedural status of the case? Two examples of the many possibilities here are "A got a verdict of ____," "B appealed the verdict to a higher court on the basis of ____," or "Plaintiff appealed from the granting of a motion to dismiss the action."

c) Issue or question
What is the central issue or question raised in this case? (There may be more than one question or issue.) For example, in People vs. Tomlins, the case briefed on the next pages, the central issue is, "Does a person have the right to kill in self-defense when attacked in his own home and when safe retreat is available?"

d) Decision of the court

1) What is the conclusion or holding of the court? (The "court" in some cases will be one judge; in other cases, as many as nine judges.)

2) By what reasoning did the court arrive at its conclusion?

3) What is the rule of law on which the conclusion is based? (The rule of law usually will be the answer to the central issue or question; it is the legal principle on which the case stands or that it follows.)

e) Your critical questions or comments
What do you think about the case?

4. **Your notes for each case should be limited to one side of one page or card, and they should have generally the same structure.**

The structure should consist primarily of a) facts, b) the nature of the action and procedural status, c) issue or question, d) decision of the court, and e) your critical questions or comments – so that you can quickly compare your notes from many similar cases, and draw conclusions about a particular body of law.

5. **Buy a legal dictionary.**

    For precise definitions of terms that you will encounter in your reading and need to use in your writing, consult a dictionary such as Mellinkoff's *Dictionary of American Legal Usage* (Eagan, MN: West Publishing Corporation, 1992).

Once you have developed familiarity with court opinions, you should be able to read and take notes according to an order or system that is related to your specific purpose for reading a case.

Some law schools may have orientation days that include presentations or materials regarding effective ways to read legal cases. Such materials have been developed by Professor Louis B. Schwartz, formerly of the University of Pennsylvania and now of Hastings College of the Law in San Francisco. In his mimeographed booklet, "Studying Law for Fun and Profit" (1978), Professor Schwartz describes the goals of legal education:

Legal education aims to develop critical judgment and a particular set of professional skills. Among these skills are careful reading and precise writing, the power to analyze an argument, differentiating facts from opinion, and recognizing the basic premise or assumption from which the argument proceeds.

In the extract below, Professor Schwartz provides a sample of appropriate note-taking from a legal case, which in part illustrates the above recommendations and in part illustrates that good note-taking by law students can vary slightly so long as the focus is on the *legal issues* involved in the case.

People vs. Tomlins (N.Y. 1914)

Facts: T shot his son in their home. Testified he acted in s.d. and provoked by blows. Judge charged df. had a duty to retreat if possible where there was a reasonable safe means of escape, rather than kill. Jury conv. T of 1st deg. murder.

Question on Appeal: Did the court commit reversible error in so instructing?

Decision and Reasons: Rev'd. because of erroneous instr. No duty to retreat when attacked in one's home. "Flight is for sanctuary and shelter, and shelter, if not sanctuary, is in the home." Ct. follows Ala. decision in holding that it makes no difference whether attacker was another occupant rather than intruder. Dictum that duty to retreat exists only in "sudden affrays."

Error held rev'bl. even tho def. atty. did not object, since charge in effect deprived T of jury trial. Statute allows reversal in capital case where "justice requires."

Rule: Not criminal to kill in s.d. when attacked in one's own home even if safe retreat available and even if attacker also lives in same home.

Comment: Wouldn't more lives be saved if retreat were required in such situations? Query as to duty to retreat only in "sudden affrays." Maybe ruling requiring retreat from murderous attack when [person] has means of defense is inconsistent with human nature.

Professor Schwartz then comments on these notes as follows:

> *Note use of abbreviations to save time. The "Question on Appeal" and "Rule" are not absolutely essential since it is fairly obvious, from the facts and the decision, what the questions are and what rule the case could be cited for. Note the quoted words from Cardozo's opinion (under "Decisions and Reasons"). This was not essential either, but occasionally it is worth taking note of a striking statement that embodies the rule of policy that seems to influence the court. The "Comment" heading is where you put your own original reaction to the decision. Always carry your thinking about a case far enough to have a definite sense of agreement or disagreement with the court's judgment. Test the court's "rule" by thinking of cases where literal application would make it absurd. Formulate an alternative rule that might be enacted by statute. Test its possibilities for absurd applications.*

Be sure to note reference to statutes in an opinion. Did the language of the statute compel the judge to decide as he did? Was the statute intended to codify the common law or to change it? Which were the crucial words that the Court had to interpret?

The foregoing recommendations for reading and note-taking in studying poetry or the law are examples of the recommendations you can find for any genre or discipline if you consult an expert or an introductory text by an expert in the field. Keep in mind that notes from the same material could be taken according to different organizations or systems, depending upon your academic or personal purposes beyond basic comprehension. In fact, changing the organization or system can be valuable in itself, because it can result in your having a new understanding of, or realization about, the subject.

Remember that your business in reading or in conversation, especially on the subject of natural, moral, or divine science, is not merely to know the opinion of the author or speaker, for this is but the mere knowledge of history; but your chief business is to consider whether their opinions are right or no, and to improve your own solid knowledge of that subject by meditation on the themes of their writing or discourse. Deal freely with every author you read, and yield up your assent only to evidence and just reasoning on the subject.

Isaac Watts, 1741

Questioning to encourage critical and creative reading

The following questions can serve as a useful stock from which to draw in thinking about and taking notes on expository material (material that presents, explains, interprets information or ideas). To increase your interest, attention, and memory, your initial question should be, "What in this material is of particular interest to me?"

1. **Critical questions: analysis**

   a) What authority or credentials does the author bring to the subject?

   b) Is the date of publication or copyright significant for my interpreting this author's words?

   c) What does the author state?

   d) What does the author imply? Assume?

   e) Is the argument valid (internally consistent, logical, the conclusions following from the premises)?

   f) Is the argument reliable (supported by evidence, authentic)?

   g) Does the form strengthen or support the content (by being clear, concise, coherent)?

2. **Creative questions: synthesis and elaboration**

   a) How does the material relate to:

      1) my own experience, opinion, knowledge?

      2) other sources, oral or written, on a similar subject

         — from other schools or other fields?

         — based on other paradigms, models, or theories?

         — by other authors in the same school or field?

   b) What additions can I think of (improvements, more evidence, additional arguments, new questions)?

3. Creative questions: applications

   a) What applications can I think of?

   b) For whom might this have value?

   c) How can this change me?

After taking notes based on questions such as the above, select an idea from your notes that you would like to develop, or a thesis that you would like to defend. Whether or not you actually make the oral or written presentation, simply having thought about the material so critically and creatively will help you remember it better and longer.

Minding metaphors

Metaphors, one of the "devices of compression" characteristic of poetry, may be found in any writing except purely scientific or mathematical material. Metaphors may cause comprehension problems for readers who are not alert to this way of conveying meaning.

A metaphor (derived from the Greek words for "beyond" – *meta*, and "bear" or "carry" – *phor*) bears meaning beyond the literal level. If you think of the same word as it might be found in purely scientific and in purely poetic material, you are likely to appreciate more fully the way that a metaphor bears meaning.

Consider the differences between the meaning of words such as "light" and "fire" in scientific material and the meaning of the same words in poetry.

In scientific material:

> *The sun is our most important source of light.*
> *Fire is the heat and light that come from burning substances.*

In a poem by Dylan Thomas:

> *Do not go gentle into that good night,*
> *Rage, rage against the dying of the light.*

In a poem by John Masefield:

> *Be with me, Beauty, for the fire is dying;*
> *My dog and I are old, too old for roving... .*
> *Only stay with me while the mind remembers*
> *The beauty of fire from the beauty of embers.*

With these quotations in view, consider language as a continuum from the purely scientific to the purely poetic, as shown in the following figure.

A CONTINUUM OF LANGUAGE

|—————————————————————|—————————————————————|

Purely scientific   **Purely poetic**

One word: One meaning   **One word: Many meanings**
1. states   1. suggests
2. denotes   2. connotes
3. appeals to intellect   3. appeals to senses,
   primarily   emotions, intellect,
                                      imagination

The continuum of language shown suggests that written material
may be located at any point from the purely scientific to the purely poetic; that is, it may be more or less scientific or poetic. In
reading any material, especially material in a genre or discipline
new to you, be alert to metaphors and the meanings they convey.
Also notice similes, which are figures of comparison like metaphors but are usually introduced by the words "as" or "like."

· ·

*Be alert to metaphors
and the meanings they convey.*

▬▬▬▬▬▬▬▬▬▬

Here are examples of metaphors and similes found in material
representative of several disciplines:

History

> *A historian should yield himself to his subject, become
> immersed in the place and period of his choice, standing
> apart from it now and then for a fresh view; as a navigator,
> after taking soundings off a strange coast, retires to peruse
> his charts and then emerges to give the necessary orders to
> continue the voyage safely.*
>
> Samuel E. Morison, in *Vistas of History*

Psychiatry

> *The problem of anxiety neurosis may be epitomized*
> *metaphorically as an overactive "alarm system." The anx-*
> *ious patient is so keyed to the possibility of harm that he is*
> *constantly warning himself about potential dangers....*
> *Almost any stimulus may be sufficient to trip off the warn-*
> *ing system and create a "false alarm." The consequence... is*
> *that the patient does experience harm – he is in a constant*
> *state of anxiety.*

> Aaron T. Beck, in *Cognitive Therapy and the*
> *Emotional Disorders*

Linguistics

> *A game of chess is like an artificial realization of what lan-*
> *guage offers in a natural form... a state of the set of chess-*
> *men corresponds closely to a state of language. The respec-*
> *tive value of the pieces depends on their position on the*
> *chessboard just as each linguistic term derives its value from*
> *its opposition to all other terms.*

> Ferdinand de Saussure, in *Courses in General*
> *Linguistics*

In addition to such incidental metaphors and similes, basic
and pervasive metaphors can be found in almost every field. For
example, in the field of English literature, the metaphor of a
plant (usually a tree) has been used to convey the concept of
"organic form." According to the theory of organic form, a work
of art "grows like a living organism, its parts inseparable and
indivisible, and the whole being greater than the sum of its
parts...." (C. Hugh Holman, in *A Handbook to Literature)*.

Minding the metaphor of a tree can be helpful in trying to
analyze a literary work. In the field of psychology, perhaps the
most well-known metaphor is that of the computer as an infor-
mation-processing mechanism comparable to the human mind.
In education, the process of education in general (and reading in
particular) has for centuries been compared to nourishment, as

it is in this quotation from Alfred North Whitehead *(The Aims of Education and Other Essays):*

> *It must never be forgotten that education is not a process of packing articles in a trunk.... Its nearest analogue is the assimilation of food by a living organism: and we all know how necessary to health is palatable food under suitable conditions. When you have put your boots in a trunk, they will stay there till you take them out again; but this is not at all the case if you feed a child with the wrong food.*

8

Adapting Recommendations in this Book to Studying Business Cases

If you read this book critically and creatively, you can adapt and apply its recommendations for reading specialized material, or for other purposes not mentioned in this book. A good example is studying business cases.

The term "case," as used here, refers to a kind of professional writing. Business cases differ from legal cases in their form and substance, and in their purpose for the reader. Therefore, this book's section on reading legal cases is limited in its applicability to reading business cases. Legal cases are the written opinions of courts, that is, judges. In writing or reviewing cases, judges must follow formal conventions and strict standards, such as the precedents established by earlier cases. Legal cases are read by law students and by practicing lawyers, who must keep up with developments in their fields of legal practice.

Business cases, on the other hand, are published primarily in textbooks for business students. They represent the textbook writer's version of what happened in a particular business situation, which may be actual or hypothetical, and they are presented as problems for business students to analyze. Although business professionals need to be able to analyze situations in their own businesses and need to keep up in their fields by reading business journals, they generally do not need to read business cases unless they take a course for their continuing professional education.

Guidelines that are directly applicable for reading business cases can be found in several sections of this book. The section on studying legal cases is applicable to business cases primarily regarding item 2b, below.

To study business cases:

1. **Preview, read, and take notes, as described in "Reading expository material for study purposes" (chapter 6), and chapter 7.**

2. **Read critically and creatively, as described in "Questioning to encourage critical and creative reading" (chapter 7).**

    a) To read business cases critically, identify and analyze the most pertinent facts and numbers, which may be both the information given in the case and the information that you infer from studying it.

    b) To read business cases creatively, ask yourself, "What are the issues in this case?" "What courses of action might be the most appropriate?" "What might be some social consequences, short-range and long-range, of each possible course of action?"

    c) In making notes about the case, include specific examples that support your points, as recommended in chapters 13 and 15. Draw your examples not only from the business case itself, but also from related sources and from your own experiences.

3. **Prepare to discuss the case in a school or work setting by reviewing the key points in your critical and creative notes.**

For more comprehensive recommendations about analyzing business cases, consult Robert Ronstadt's *The Art of Case Analysis: A Guide to the Diagnosis of Business Situations,* 3rd ed. (Dana Point, CA: Lord, 1994).

Many of the questions useful in analyzing business cases can also be applied productively to a current business problem or business opportunity of your own. While reading and discussing a business case, ask yourself questions such as "How can this change me?" "How can my own work or that of my work team on this case be more effective and efficient?" "What have I learned from this case that might help me in my current or future business positions?"

·······························

Ask yourself,
"What are the issues in this case?"

You are fortunate if you have a job in which you can directly apply to your work what you are learning through your studying. To learn more effectively, make lists that will help you plan to apply some of the concepts, principles, and skills you are learning. The lists may include specific tasks or steps you could undertake, the problems and opportunities you might encounter, and—noted in a column alongside those lists—the names of people who might help or hinder you in your efforts.*

* These last two paragraphs are based on my consultation with Dr. Diane Bradford, formerly director of, later consultant to, the Division of Executive Education at The Wharton School, University of Pennsylvania.

9

Preparing a Research Paper

To meet the due date, schedule on your calendar when you will *start* each of the following major steps. Count back from the date your paper is due, and estimate how many days you should allow for each step. Until you are experienced in preparing research papers, shorten the time for each major step by seeking help from a university writing center or a professional writing consultant. Even if you are somewhat experienced, you may benefit from consulting a book or article about ways to do advanced writing in a particular discipline.

Research

1. **Choose your topic carefully.**

    a) Jot down as many topics as you can think of related to a subject that is appropriate or actually assigned for your paper.

    b) Evaluate the topics you've listed, especially keeping in mind your genuine personal interest in each topic and its possible value for you.

    c) Limit and organize your topic before and during your research on it. To decide what to include, consider what you know and want to know about the topic, what the instructor has assigned, and how much time you have to complete the paper. Try to:

1) Build your paper around a question, for which the paper serves as a well-balanced and well-organized answer, with all the necessary evidence to support your points, or

2) Develop and defend a potent idea or thesis about the subject, with explicit references to alternative views and possibilities, which you should research carefully and present fairly.

2. **Write a list of as many questions as you can think of about your topic.**

Study the questions to

a) find possible categories that might be included in your paper;

b) eliminate questions that are likely to take you too far from your central topic.

....

Build your paper around a question... or develop and defend a potent idea or thesis about the subject.

3. **Get an overview of your topic.**

Read a general source, such as an encyclopedia article, and note names, events, terms and keywords, or ideas that you might use in your library search for specific sources.

4. **Locate and note information sources efficiently.**

a) Take advantage of library services that may be available. Use the library's printed guides, and take a tour to learn how the library is organized and whether there are any special collections or departments specifically related to your subject area.

b) Consult reference librarians for the very latest information about using electronic sources, because the information changes about every six months. The librarian might suggest recent books on this subject for you to consult. You might also want to check the Library of Congress on the Internet, or attend a library workshop on using the Internet or other specific databases. Using databases to preview or screen material that is available on your subject can save you a great amount of time. However, some other on-line searches can be very time consuming and expensive. Whether or when you should use electronic sources may depend upon how current you need the material to be.

c) Revise your list of subject headings or keywords to use in researching your topic. Ask the reference librarian about search terms to use, as well as sources to consult.

d) Locate appropriate books through the library's catalog. This may be a card catalog, an on-line (computerized) catalog, or a combination of both.

    1) From the catalog, note on separate notepad pages the author, title, location, and call number of all books that seem likely to contain useful information. In making your choices, notice the date of publication and the scope and tone indicated by the title.

    2) Find and look over each promising book to determine further its possible usefulness. Check the table of contents and the index, the qualifications of the author, and the degree of scholarship that the author demonstrates in writing about an aspect of the subject you know something about.

    3) Indicate in an upper corner of the bibliographical slip the status of the book, e.g., "not in the

library," "not useful," "being called in," or other information, and group the slips accordingly.

e) Check the periodical indexes in the reference room or on-line databases of periodical literature for current journal, magazine, and newspaper articles on your subject. This is another point at which reference librarians can help you plan your work. They can also help you learn how to do effective literature searches via computer, especially through retrieving useful and time-saving abstracts of articles.

f) Write a full bibliographical card* only for those books and periodicals from or about which you expect to take notes. Use standard bibliographical form (see 4e, p. 81). Make sure to record all the information so that you won't have to waste time backtracking later.

g) If important materials on your topic are not accessible, *consider changing your topic.*

5. Read portions of the books appropriate to the subject and make page notations and notes of your ideas about the material.

a) As you read, note the pages and parts of pages (A, B, C, D, E) from which you think you'll want to take notes when you complete most of your reading, and make these notations on the bibliographical card for the book (see chapter 5).

b) Note on separate cards each of your own original ideas regarding the subject, indicating the author and page number of the material about which you are commenting.

6. Ordinarily, do *not* take notes *yet* from the content itself.

Arrange for a conference with your professor when you have read enough to have one or two thesis ideas or questions that seem promising bases for your paper. You can save immeasurable time and effort, and insure the success

---

* Books: Author, title, edition, place of publication, publisher, date of publication.
Articles: Author, article title, periodical title, volume, date, pages.

of your paper, if you discuss your plans at this point with your professor or supervisor. During the discussion, take careful notes of any recommendations.

7. **If you have located electronic texts about your subject, view them on a library computer and, if permissible, print out copies or make notes from the parts that seem useful for your paper.**

   a) Keep in mind that only a small percentage of full-text resources are available in electronic format so far. (In the field of literature, an extraordinary example of such texts is the electronic "variorum" of Mary Shelley's *Frankenstein* – all the criticism and scholarship on this literary work gathered on CD-ROM by University of Pennsylvania scholars and published by University of Pennsylvania Press.)

   b) When you've searched and previewed on the screen one or more pages pertinent to your topic, print out the pages so that you can file them with your other notes, making it easier to quote and cite sources accurately and quickly. If possible, download the pages onto a disk of your own, so that they become part of your own electronic notes that you can print out on your own printer. Libraries differ in the amount of downloading and printing they allow, in general and from particular databases.

   Caution: You may be allowed to download and print pages to keep in your own files for your own use, but copyright law prohibits you from reproducing and distributing these records except under "Fair Use" guidelines. (See Appendix A on copyright law.)

8. **Drawing from your note cards, write a tentative and very brief outline.**

9. **Take notes from your reading.**

   a) Return to the pages you've noted and, if the material still seems valuable in view of the thesis you have decided upon, take notes of some kind: summaries, quotations, or paraphrasing.

b) Use a separate card for each new idea. Note the subject in the upper right-hand corner and the author's name and the exact page reference in the upper left-hand corner.

c) In using electronic sources, make notes on your response to the material, and take notes from the material itself if you decide not to print it out. You may want to take your notes on a laptop computer.

d) Take great care to avoid plagiarism and infringement of copyright. For any and every source from which you quote or paraphrase in your paper, note the reference in a footnote or parentheses, as recommended by your instructor or style manual. For detailed guidance in avoiding copyright infringement, see a library or legal reference book, such as *Henn on Copyright Law: A Practitioner's Guide,* 3rd ed., by Harry G. Henn (New York: Practising Law Institute, 1991), brief excerpts of which are provided in the appendix of this book.

e) When you use electronic sources, you might need to modify some of the procedures for citing sources that I've described earlier in this section. In particular, you might have to cite a reference by the numbers and/or names of sections and subsections (for example, "I,6,c. The Academic Standards of the New Age"), instead of by page number, because standards about matters such as pagination for electronic manuscripts have not yet been set. Also, in noting information for a bibliography, you might have to include the database you used and even the date you used it, because the electronic text might be continually open to revision.

10. **For full information on using the World Wide Web for research purposes, consult a book on the subject.**

Dawn Rodrigues's *The Research Paper and the World Wide Web* (Upper Saddle River, NJ: Prentice Hall, 1997), for example, can give you detailed instructions about navigating the Web, finding library resources on it, using its various research tools, organizing your notes on it, citing your sources, and honoring copyrights.

11. **Use your ingenuity to discover other possible sources of information in addition to books, periodicals, and various electronic sources.**

   If you know people who are well informed on your subject, communicate with them by mail, e-mail, the Internet, by telephone, or in person. In your research paper, cite the name of the person and the date and the means of communication.

12. **Throughout the process of preparing your research paper, make notes of your critical appraisal and original ideas about the material.**

   a) Note the author and the page number or electronic location of the material you are commenting about.

   b) Keep notepad pages or index cards handy for recording ideas that may come to you in odd moments, and add these to your collection of notes.

   c) Compile clear definitions of all terms that are important to your paper.

Write

1. **First of all, use a word processor if at all possible.**

   They are invaluable aids to efficient and effective thinking and writing.

2. **Prepare a brief statement of the thesis, purpose, and/or scope of your paper.**

   This statement will serve as a point of reference that keeps you close to your subject as you write.

3. **Write a full outline, following the steps below.**

   a) Arrange your notes carefully in what seems to be an appropriate sequence.

b) Include definitions of key terms.

c) Add cards with notes of any new ideas, insights, and conclusions that come to you as you review them.

d) From your note cards, write your outline in sentence form, to insure clarity and continuity as you write your paper from it.

4. Write a first draft of your paper.

a) Review comments by professors or supervisors on your previous papers for suggestions that can improve your current paper.

b) Write point by point from your outline, reorganizing when it seems desirable. Write the introduction later if it seems difficult to express at first.

c) In footnotes or endnotes, cite all the sources of ideas and quotations not your own. (See item 9d, p. 79).

d) Choose or create graphic material such as photographs, drawings, or graphs that you can introduce or develop on your computer and print out, to support or elaborate on points you make in your paper. Cite fully the sources of all the illustrative material you use.

e) Consult a current and standard style manual for an appropriate and consistent form for your footnotes and bibliography – for example, *The MLA Handbook for Writers of Research Papers,* or *The Publication Manual of the American Psychological Association.* (See Bibliography.) If you are not sure, ask your instructor which style manual he or she prefers.

f) Strive for fluent expression, not precise diction, in the first draft; circle words that you think should be replaced in later drafts.

g) Develop a strong introduction and conclusion. The introduction should state your thesis or question clearly. The conclusion should include a brief summary and restatement of the thesis or question.

Revise

1. **After completing your first draft and making a printout, wait at least a day to allow time for mental refreshment.**

   Then reread and polish the draft.

   a) Check: Are your points clear? Does every paragraph develop the thesis? Is the progression logical and coherent? Are the headings accurate and helpful? Could a person reading your paper for the first time preview it easily? Make the changes necessary for you to answer yes to all these questions.

   b) Find the precise words to express your points.

   c) Reread parts of the paper out loud to reveal any rough spots.

   d) In a long paper, provide additional organizational aids for the reader, such as a table of contents and headings.

2. **Write a second draft of the pages that need major revision.**

   Then allow time for mental refreshment again. (Several revisions may be desirable, if time is available.)

3. **Type or print out a final draft. Proofread and correct it. Print a final copy.**

4. **Be sure to back up your computer files, print a spare, or photocopy the paper for safekeeping.**

Submit

Turn the paper in on time (or, if absolutely necessary, arrange for a new deadline that is possible for you to meet and acceptable to your professor or supervisor).

Bibliographical note: Many books about writing research papers are being revised to include procedures for using electronic sources, for example, Melissa Walker's *Writing Research Papers,*

4th ed. (Norton, 1997). There are also guides to writing in general fields, such as the social sciences, and specific fields, such as psychology. For detailed explanations of ways to cite electronic sources, refer to the Rodrigues book noted in item 10 above, or *The Chicago Manual of Style,* readily available in library reference sections.

10

Using Four Methods for Effective Study – and for Analogous Activities

Many of the preceding sections of this book referred to one or more of four basic and interdependent methods of improving reading, writing, and studying: previewing, selecting, chunking, and deep processing. (See chapter 2 for examples.)

The four methods can be used for lengthy as well as brief activities – for taking around-the-world journeys or short trips; preparing for comprehensive examinations or brief tests; writing dissertations or short papers; deciding on a career or a course; planning your retirement or a party. For an extended studying task, previewing involves carefully determining the scope of the task. Selecting and chunking involve dividing the whole into parts, deciding which tasks to work on first and which to work on most thoroughly, then grouping the tasks that are best done together. Deep processing involves studying one chunk after another, using the ways of thinking about the material that are most appropriate for each chunk and for your purposes.

Naturally, previewing, selecting, chunking, and deep processing are not always necessary or desirable. They are necessary and desirable when efficiency is important, and when the major purpose is accomplishment of some kind within limited time and in a competitive situation – the conditions of most academic and professional work. For other activities, just one or two of the methods might be desirable or useful. When you're on vacation you may enjoy simply wandering, without studying a map of the area, and when you come upon a shelf of books you may enjoy simply choosing a book on whim and wandering through it.

Here is a graphic summary of these methods.

FOUR METHODS BASIC TO EFFECTIVE STUDY

Preview
Preview books that you need to study for an exam or to write a research paper.

Preview
Preview the chapter most interesting to you or most appropriate for your purposes.

Select
Select the book most interesting or appropriate to read first, preferably one providing an overview of the subject.

Select
Select the part of the chapter most interesting or appropriate to read first.

Chunk
Chunk by grouping the books according to subject, author, or other aspect related to your purposes.

Chunk
Chunk by grouping parts of the chapter according to problems to be solved, questions to be answered, or according to sections appropriate for note-taking. Read one chunk at a time.

Process
Process the books in ways most appropriate for your purposes, such as outlining answers to anticipated exam questions or making notes for a research paper.

Process
After reading a chunk, process in the way most appropriate for your purposes—recite what you have learned, solve a problem, answer a question, note ideas about the material, or mark page numbers from which to take more detailed notes at another time.

11

Strengthening Vocabulary as a Habit or Hobby

1. **When reading or listening, write down every unfamiliar word you encounter.**

   a) Note the phrase in which you found the word (or the page and part of page—indicated by A, B, C, D, E— noting the phrase later).

   b) Guess the meaning from the context of the word and from structural clues, but do *not* write down your guess. Read on.

2. **After collecting a number of words, note on an index card, using a good dictionary,* the following information.**

   a) any part of the pronunciation you're not sure about

   b) phrase in which you found the word (with quotation marks)

   c) derivation, if it will help you remember the meaning

   d) meaning that is appropriate for the context quoted

   e) other useful meanings, synonyms, and antonyms

   f) definitions of unfamiliar synonyms or antonyms (to clarify any subtle differences between these and the key word)

---

* For studying in your major field or at a level above that of an introductory course in a discipline new to you, you should own a current, authoritative dictionary specific to the field; for example, in literature, William Harmon and C. Hugh Holman's *Handbook to Literature,* 7th ed. (Macmillan: New York, 1997).

g) other forms of the word, such as in other parts of speech, or in idioms

h) the word itself on the back of the card for drill purposes.

3. **Study new words in odd moments, thinking of ways you might use them in various contexts. For each word:**

a) study the spelling, definition, and any other information you have noted about the word;

· ·

Study new words in odd moments, thinking of ways you might use them in various contexts.

b) write the word from memory, and check immediately for accuracy;

c) recite the definition and other information from memory, and check immediately for accuracy.

Here are two examples of vocabulary cards that I have accumulated since I began the hobby of word-collecting years ago. I include them here to illustrate that note-taking about words can be very brief, including only information that will help you understand, remember, and want to use the word.

> *euphoric*
>
> *"The experience (Harvard) tends to be more astringent than euphoric"*
>
> *From Greek "eu" = well + "phoric" = to bear*
>
> *"giving a sense of well-being and buoyancy; incapable of depression or readily shaking it."*

heuristic

– "start with it as a heuristic principle."

– "the use of the heuristic hunch"

From Greek, "to discover" – EUREKA!

"serving to find out (for oneself), such as an educational system in which students are trained to find out things for themselves."

12

Learning a Foreign Language

In learning a foreign language, you can apply or adapt many of the ideas in the preceding chapters, especially chapter 3, "Mastering textbook material" in chapter 6, and chapter 11. Other sections of this book can also help you read, write, and study in a foreign language as well as in your native language.

However, learning a foreign language requires additional methods and efforts:

1. Use audiotapes regularly; these accompany most textbooks for foreign-language study.

2. Study frequently—six days a week—in short, intensive sessions.

3. In learning new words, cluster or group about five words that are related in some way, then study the words one cluster at a time.

4. Study most intensively the words and phrases that you find most difficult to remember.

    a) Use as many senses, in as many ways as you can, while studying. For example: write the word or phrase while looking at it and saying it, think about its parts and its meaning, write it again while saying it but not looking at it, check to see if you got it right. Repeat this process several times.

    b) Look for some way to relate the difficult word to some-

thing familiar, and think of this relationship as you continue
to rehearse the word.

c) Write the word or phrase on index cards, as described in
chapter 11, and review the cards aloud several times a
day in odd moments and before you go to sleep the night
before a test.

5. **Read passages for their general meaning, without concern
for recognizing every word.**

When you encounter an unfamiliar word, write it on a 3-by-
5-inch memo page or index card. When you have finished
reading the passage, decide which words you need to learn,
and proceed to learn them by following the method
described above.

6. **Look for opportunities to use the foreign language in real-life
situations or with other students of the language.**

Use it for greetings and for expressing ideas and thoughts
that are important to you. Rehearse for real-life use by
imagining situations that involve several speakers, and play
all the roles. Read current foreign-language newspapers and
magazines, and see foreign language films. Learn songs in
the language and sing them aloud. Try to visit places where
the language is spoken. Such real-life use can enhance your
motivation and increase your learning in ways no other
method can.

· ·

*Look for opportunities
to use the foreign language
in real-life situations.*

If you have severe problems mastering a foreign language, you
might need special help. Usually this involves more repetition and

more time to learn the language. Seek help through your instructor, the faculty member responsible for language instruction in your school, a learning center, and/or an office for students with disabilities (including learning disabilities).

13

Improving Writing

If you look back in this book, you will see that there is only one section, "Preparing a Research Paper," that is specifically about writing. The rest of the sections are more directly about reading. But reading, writing, speaking, and listening are so closely related that some of the ways to improve each can also be applied to improving the others.

The relationships between reading and writing, and the ways to improve them, can be made clearer by using the same terms for their similar aspects. For example, we could say that in reading expository writing we look for a thesis statement and ways by which it is supported, while in writing we develop a thesis statement and ways to support it. Similarly, we could use the terms *previewing, selecting, chunking,* and *deep processing,* which are described as ways to improve reading (see chapter 10), in describing ways to improve writing.

Here, then, are specific suggestions for ways you can improve your writing in terms of the ways recommended for improving reading. In writing as in reading, the activities are interrelated or overlap. While reading is like eating a dinner, writing is like creating a dinner. It usually involves some step-by-step activities, but mostly it involves back-and-forth considering and doing, reconsidering and revising, until just before the guests sit down to eat.

Prepare to write

1. **If the genre in which you are writing is unfamiliar to you,**

ask your instructor, a librarian, or another authority to recommend a model of the genre that you can examine.

2. **Collect as much material as you can about your subject before you try to write a first draft.**

For a research paper, this should involve the kind of reading and note-taking described in chapter 9.

3. **Make notes of your ideas and observations.**

To save time, write each idea or observation on separate small pages or cards, so that you can arrange and rearrange them before you write your first draft.

4. **As you make notes, try to conceive questions or ideas that might guide your notetaking, and that ultimately might unify the paper you need to write.**

Preview

Previewing is helpful at several times during the writing process, but especially before you write your first draft – after you've collected as much material as you can.

1. **Preview or review freshly all the notes you have accumulated on your subject.**

2. **Look for relationships among the notes and ideas you have collected,**

which might help you organize your paper as an answer to one major question or in support of one potent idea or thesis that you conceive.

Select and chunk

Sort and group your notes according to the relationships you see as you preview:

1. **Select by deciding on a question or thesis and the most promising way to answer or support it.**

2. **Select the audience for whom you want to write, and keep that audience in mind as you write and revise.**

    This helps to make what you write and how you write it as appropriate as possible. In an academic situation, the audience is mainly your instructor; keep your particular instructor in mind.

3. **Select from your notes all those that are appropriate for the question or thesis and the audience you have selected.**

4. **Chunk by sketching a pattern—a map or an outline—to represent your decisions about how you will group and arrange your ideas.**

5. **Write your outline in full sentences.**

    These sentences should be the main assertions that you feel ready to make in answer to your question or in support of your thesis. Keep in mind that you may change these assertions as you continue to write.

Process deeply

1. **Write your paper following your map or outline and your notes.**

    Feel free to reconceive and reorder your ideas as you see new relationships, or perhaps even discover a better question or a more potent thesis.

2. **Support your points with carefully chosen examples, or clarify them through analogies or metaphors (implied analogies).**

3. **You will have processed deeply in preparing to write, and in previewing, selecting, and chunking.**

    You will be continuing to process deeply as you write, as you revise your paper, and as you read your finished product. Because deep processing occurs throughout the writing process, writing is regarded as a way of knowing or getting to know, not just a way of telling.

· ·

Writing is regarded as a way of knowing... not just a way of telling.

4. **Revise your draft and rewrite until you feel satisfied enough with your product to show it to a friend.**

5. **Ask your friend to respond to a particular part of your writing that you are concerned about.**

   Discuss with your friend what questions he or she has about what you've written, and what questions other readers might be expected to have about it. Revise your writing in light of any of the friend's suggestions that seem appropriate to you.

6. **In some schools or classes, this sort of sharing of papers may not be appropriate or acceptable.**

   When this is the case, allow several days between each rereading of your drafts, and read them as if you were the audience for whom you have written.

7. **Examine each draft for ways to make it more easily previewable by your readers, and clearer and more readable in style.**

8. **Edit your final draft: weed out redundancies, imprecisions, and errors in grammar or spelling.**

   Realize that you will find ways to improve your paper whenever you reread it; it will never be perfect, and it need not be. Just do your best in the time you have.

To illustrate the process I have recommended, I'll describe how I wrote these pages.

To prepare to write them, I noted on 3-by-5-inch memo pages all the ideas that came to my mind about ways to write more effectively, particularly for academic or professional purposes. I read or reviewed a half dozen books about writing, noting pages and parts of pages from which I might want to take notes eventually. As I read, I noted my own new ideas about my subject immediately, each idea on a separate memo page.

When I felt I had done enough reading or reviewing for my purposes, I returned to my notations of pages and parts of pages, and made notes from each book on separate 3-by-5-inch pages, noting the author and page number in the upper left-hand corner.

When I felt I had accumulated enough notes and ideas, I previewed (reviewed freshly) all my notes, looking for relationships among them and ways that they might best be arranged to answer the question, "What suggestions should I give to students for improving the way they go about their writing?" As I previewed, I wrote additional notes when new ideas occurred to me. I also began to sort the note pages into stacks, and I jotted down headings for each stack. Here are the headings I jotted down:

> *Reading related to writing*
>
> *Previewing*
>
> *Selecting*
>
> *Chunking*
>
> *Deep processing*
>
> *Books about improving writing*

Then I wrote a first draft of the assertions I felt I could make, and ways I might support the assertions. Here's what I wrote:

> *As reading and writing are related,*
> *so are ways to improve them*
>
> *Previewing, selecting, chunking, and deep processing can be*
> *applied to writing as well as to reading*

Explain application

Illustrate

Read books about improving writing.

Following this rough outline and my matching stacks of notes, I wrote a first draft. I set the draft aside for about a week. When I reread the draft I marked revisions directly on it. A week later I copied the revised draft, editing as I typed.

I read the draft aloud to myself and made more changes. I duplicated the revised second draft so that I could show it to one of my colleagues, Susan L. Lytle. She suggested that I revise the pages to build up the part about preparing to write, making more statements about improving writing, and that I weed out some of the details of my explanation. She also suggested that I illustrate the process I was recommending by using some writing other than the pages themselves. I followed the first three suggestions, but I decided not to follow the last one.

In my first draft, I realized to my surprise that I had forgotten my main audience. I was writing for teachers, who have been the audience for most of my professional writing, rather than students. When I wrote the second draft I kept in mind an audience of students or a particular student. I also kept in mind the structure and metaphors I had used for the earlier draft. I typed a third draft of the pages, edited it briefly, and read it out loud to myself. I made additional changes that were indicted by the way the words sounded when I read them out loud.

I duplicated the third draft to show to several more of my colleagues. They pointed out sentences that I could make clearer or more concise.

I typed a fourth draft and sent this to my editor, Robert W. Boynton. Bob suggested that I be more realistic or frank in making some of my points. For example, I should admit that the only audience for most student writing "is the teacher, unfortunately."

The result of the process I have just described is the section that you are reading now.

Learning to use a word processor, which I did between the second and third editions of this book, has enhanced my writing. Using it saves immeasurable time, and makes the writing process so much more pleasurable and the product so much more readable that it helps prevent procrastination and increases concentration.

Buy or rent a word processor if you can, or arrange to use one regularly through the computer resource center at your school, office, or copy store.

Since I first wrote this chapter, five years ago, computer technology has developed more and more rapidly and is likely to continue doing so. With the Internet we can communicate with people all over the world, and with laptop computers we can omit some of the paper-and-pencil steps that I describe above. With computer graphics we can learn better, as well as illustrate better, the subjects of our papers. For two reasons I have maintained my description of the way I wrote this section: 1) the process is still useful, especially for researchers who may not always have access to electronic resources; and 2) the basic ideas I utilized are readily applicable to new resources and technology.

For more ideas about ways to improve your writing, look for books on the subject in libraries or bookstores, especially college bookstores on shelves labeled for English composition courses, and consult writing teachers for their recommendations.

Here are some books about improving writing that I recommend:

> Belanoff, Pat, et al. *The Right Handbook,* 2nd rev. ed. Portsmouth, NH: Boynton/Cook, 1992.

> Berthoff, Ann E., with James Stephens. *Forming/Thinking/Writing,* 2nd ed. Portsmouth, NH: Heinemann-Boynton/Cook, 1988.

> Elbow, Peter. *Writing Without Teachers,* 2nd ed. New York: Oxford University Press, 1998.

> Flower, Linda. *Problem Solving Strategies for Writing,* 5th ed. San Diego: Harcourt, 1999 (expected).

Kaye, Sanford. *Writing Under Pressure: The Quick Writing Process*. New York: Oxford University Press, 1989.

Macrorie, Ken. *The I-Search Paper*. Portsmouth, NH: Heinemann-Boynton/Cook, 1988.

Murray, Donald M. *Expecting the Unexpected: Teaching Myself—and Others—to Read and Write*. Portsmouth, NH: Heinemann-Boynton-Cook, 1989.

Williams, Joseph. *Style: Toward Clarity and Grace*. Chicago: University of Chicago Press, 1995.

14

Preparing for Examinations

The best preparation for examinations is regular study, including reviewing and learning class notes after every lecture or two, mastering each textbook assignment upon first reading it, and using other study strategies described in earlier sections of this book.

Special review, beginning at least a few days before the exam, is also necessary. The general recommendations in chapter 3 support the detailed procedures listed below.

....

The best preparation
for examinations is regular study.

1. **Plan a realistic study schedule and stick to it as closely as possible.**

   a) Decide how much material you must review and approximately how long one unit of it will take. Divide the number of units over the time available and note this on your calendar.

   b) Distribute your study time over at least two sessions for minor tests and at least four sessions for major exams. Review periods should be relatively brief, because recalling and organizing ideas is so fatiguing that efficiency usually decreases rapidly after about an hour of review.

2. **Keep paper handy for noting any ideas or feelings that occur to you about problems or plans in other areas of your life; but wait until a study break to think more about them. (See chapter 16.)**

3. **Study *actively*.**

   a) Begin by quickly previewing all your class notes and making a one-page outline (a table of contents) for them.

   b) Study as a unit each subject within the course – for example, all your notes from all sources on the same subject.

      1) Treat your class notes as you would treat a textbook chapter. After reviewing your table of contents, review and recite one section (one chunk) at a time.

      2) Review your one-page outline for each textbook chapter, and then recite or write briefly from memory. Reread portions of the textbook only if you can't remember the supporting details well; they should come to your mind as you encounter each cue on your outline.

      3) Prepare and study a master outline of important aspects of the subject for which lectures, textbooks, and supplementary reading interrelate.

   c) Create graphic aids to help you understand and remember the material: perhaps a time line, an outline map, or a model of a theory.

   d) While reading and reviewing, build a list of page and part-of-page references (A, B, C, D, E) about major terms or concepts. In reviewing for exams, take notes from these page references on separate notepad pages. Arrange the pages for each term or concept in an order that will help you develop a clear and comprehensive definition.

e) Build a list of terms, using indentation to show relationships among them. Fold the list in half lengthwise, and think about the definition of each term. For definitions you find hard to remember, write them briefly on the right-hand side of the list.

f) Avoid artificial (that is, insignificant) mnemonic (memory) devices, because these cannot help you understand the material. Instead, group key terms or ideas in significant ways. See examples of both significant and insignificant mnemonic devices at the end of this chapter.

g) Review the notes you made during your regular study, in answer to critical and creative questions like those recommended near the end of chapter 7, and write down any questions or ideas that come to your mind about the material you are reviewing.

   1) In particular, experiment with changing your point of view on the subject by using your imagination and your knowledge of controversies in the field.

   2) Make notes of your new insights.

· ·

Create graphic aids to help you understand and remember the material: perhaps a time line, an outline map, or a model of a theory.

h) For an essay exam, make up exam questions or ask your professor about old exam questions that might be available. No later than two days before the exam, think through or roughly outline your answers to the questions.

1) Anticipate one or two very broad questions that the instructor might ask. As you review your notes, write down points and pages appropriate for an answer to the question(s).

2) Cooperate with a friend in making up and exchanging more limited (and more likely) exam questions; in a dress-rehearsal situation, outline your answers to the friend's questions; later, discuss your answers with your friend.

3) Build a structure by which to recall key ideas that you are likely to need quickly – for example, the elements to consider in analyzing a poem or painting, or the factors to consider in analyzing a problem in economics.

i) Pretend to teach, or actually arrange to tutor, portions of the subject on which you will be examined. Tutoring usually results in the teacher learning even more than the student (some of the probable reasons may be found in chapter 3).

4. **Allow time to pay special attention to the parts of the material that you have found hardest.**

a) Testing yourself will help you find your weak spots; work on those most.

b) Just before going to sleep on the night before the exam, review the hardest parts, your master outlines, and your outlines of answers to the questions that you have anticipated.

5. **Get ample sleep two nights before the exam (in case you have any problem sleeping the next night), as well as the night before the exam (so that you can remember and think as clearly as possible while taking the exam).**

Rest assured that you will be expected to have thought critically and creatively about the subject matter of the course before you take the examination. Having thought and rest-ed, you will feel more confident in facing an essay exam that includes questions like "Shakespeare and the common people. Discuss." or "The French Revolution. Who won?"

Talking over the things which you have read with your companions on the first proper opportunity you have for it, is a most useful manner of review or repetition, in order to fix them upon the mind. Teach them to your younger friends, in order to establish your own knowledge while you communicate it to them. The animal powers of your tongue and of your ear, as well as your intellectual facilities, will all join together to help the memory. Hermetus studied hard in a remote corner of the land, and in solitude, yet he became a very learned man. He seldom was so happy as to enjoy suitable society at home, and therefore he talked over to the fields and the woods in the evening what he had been reading in the day....

Isaac Watts, 1741

An example of grouping ideas in significant ways

Imagine that you have to learn in detail the psychology of Abraham Maslow, and that you are studying the graphic aid in *The Third Force: The Psychology of Abraham Maslow** reprinted below. To remember the sixteen "growth needs," you should look for a basis of clustering or grouping the terms that is consistent with Maslow's psychology. You should avoid grouping on

* Frank Goble, *The Third Force: The Psychology of Abraham Maslow*, p. 52. Copyright © 1970 by Thomas Jefferson Research Center. Reprinted by permission of Viking Penguin, a division of Penguin Books USA, Inc.

insignificant bases such as alphabetizing, common suffixes, or forming a sentence from words that begin with the first letter of each of the growth needs.

How might you cluster or group the growth needs then? Realizing that, according to Maslow's theories, growth needs are

1. *nonhierarchical (that is, with no particular order of precedence)*

2. *derived from Maslow's study of individuals who seem to have achieved "self-actualization"*

you could group the growth needs in fours according to your own conception of related needs or characteristics, and then think of someone you know who seems to exemplify each of the four groups.

(1)	(2)	(3)	(4)
Truth	Aliveness	Necessity	Completion
Goodness	Individuality	Justice	Simplicity
Beauty	Richness	Order	Effortlessness
Perfection	Playfulness	Self-sufficiency	Meaningfulness

Exemplified by

1) _____ 2) _____ 3) _____ 4) _____

To recall the growth needs, you would then simply recall the four individuals you know who exemplify the characteristics; by association, you would remember the groups of related terms (needs/characteristics) that you have identified with the four individuals. By studying this way, you would not only remember the sixteen growth needs but also better understand the psychological theory of Abraham Maslow.

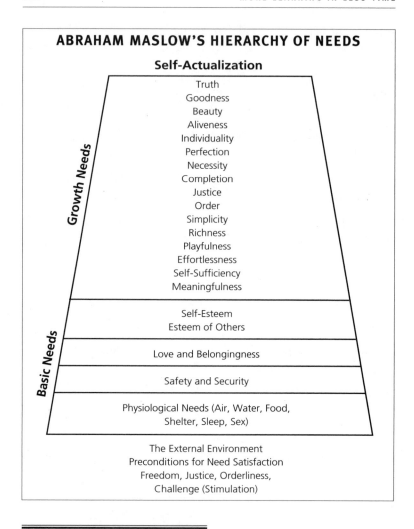

Whatsoever you would trust to your memory let it be disposed in a proper method, connected well together, and referred to distinct and particular heads or classes both general and particular.

Isaac Watts, 1741

15

Taking Examinations

Essay examinations

1. **Prepare to begin.**

   Make all your muscles tense, and then relax them quickly. Take several slow, deep breaths through your nose. Check the time, and ask whether it will be announced at all during the exam.

2. **Underline key words in the directions and questions.**

   This will focus your thinking, help you keep calm, and prevent you from trying to write before you are settled and organized.

3. **Read through all of the questions, and jot down a few words that come to mind about each question you plan to answer (if there is a choice).**

4. **Budget your time.**

   a) Consider the number of points given for each question, if this information is stated.

   b) Decide how much time you should allot for each answer, taking into consideration your knowledge of the subject and the number of points given.

   c) Allow time for a rough outline before writing each answer and for proofreading after completing the exam.

5. **Usually, answer the easiest question (or second easiest) first.**

   This will increase your confidence and give you more time to recall answers for the harder questions.

6. **Jot down a rough outline from which to write your answer for each question.**

   a) In a column, write key words and phrases related to points that you remember from lectures and from your reading and thinking for the course.

   b) Then think beyond these first ideas to new ideas that occur to you in response to the question; these ideas may be based upon your own experiences and interests as well as on the lectures and readings for the course.

   c) Number your ideas in the most appropriate order for your answer.

   d) If you run out of time in answering the question, copy the ideas from your outline to complete your answer briefly.

   ....

   Read through all of the questions; jot down a few words that come to mind about each question you plan to answer.

7. **Take care to answer precisely the question asked.**

   a) Notice especially the limitation stressed by the instruction verb (list, analyze, compare).

   b) Form the first sentence by turning the question into a statement or by writing a thesis sentence that you will support with specific examples or evidence.

c) Include a time frame, indicating, for example, whether a historical movement extended over decades or centuries.

d) When in doubt, qualify your answers by using approximate times or dates and by including qualifying words (for example, "some," "most," "usually," or "occasionally") in your statements.

e) Underline the key phrases in your answer, so that the hurried exam reader will not miss a single one of them.

8. **Begin a new paragraph for each point on your outline.**

9. **Support your main points with carefully chosen evidence or examples.**

10. **Abbreviate long names or terms that you will need to repeat frequently,**

and include a code at the top of the page on which you first use the abbreviation

(for example, T = Tchaikovsky; Rev'n = Revolution; onom. = onomatopoeia).

11. **Write clearly, concisely, and legibly.**

(If you like, inquire in advance about the possibility of typing or word–processing your exam.)

12. **Leave a space after each paragraph to allow for possible additions when you proofread.**

Or write your answers only on the front side of each page so that you can insert additions on the back if this is permitted.

13. **Proofread your answer.**

14. **After your exam is returned to you, use it to determine how to study for and take future exams more successfully.**

Sample essay question and answer

If you were given an examination on the material in this book, an appropriate question might be this one:

What advice would you give a friend who asks you for help with a serious problem – the tendency to panic at exam times?

On a separate piece of paper, follow steps 6 through 13 for taking essay examinations, then compare what you've written with the sample essay illustrated below:

[Question rephrased in opening statement:]

> If a friend asked me for advice about his problem of panicking at exam time, this is what I would tell him.

[Question interpreted broadly:]

> Consider yourself preparing for exams from the first day of class. Learn each chunk of new material as you encounter it. For example, learn lecture notes within 24 hours after every class. Preview all nonfiction material recommended, and read it selectively; delay taking notes about the content (noting instead pages and parts of pages you may return to for note taking), but note immediately your own ideas about the material. Preview required textbook chapters, and prepare a one-page outline of each chapter as you read it.

[Space left between paragraphs:]

> Plan a special review several days before the exam. Begin by building a table of contents for your class notes. Plan your study time by estimating how much time you'll need to review one chunk, and multiply by the number of chunks you have.

> Write on your calendar when you should study each chunk, counting back from the date the exam is scheduled. Study actively. For example, create

graphic aids, and formulate answers to anticipated exam questions as you study. Two nights (at least) before the exam, exchange anticipated questions with a friend, and outline your answers to unfamiliar questions. In this way you'll be having almost a dress rehearsal of the exam. The night before the exam, get enough sleep so that you will feel as alert and able to cope as possible.

[Main points underlined:]

Take precautions in taking the exam. Underline key words in the directions and in the questions, to calm your nerves and keep you from starting to write before you're ready. Budget your time, allowing first for a rough outline of your answer, and last for proofreading. Skip lines after each paragraph to allow space for inserting any new ideas you think of during proofreading.

Take advantage of professional counseling, or university services such as workshops, to help in controlling test anxiety. For this to be most effective, do it at least two months before your exams.

[Main points summarized – including a point that goes beyond the recommendations in this book. (See 6b, above.):]

Briefly then, overcoming panic at exam time is likely to require regular study from the very beginning of the course, special preparation several days in advance of the exam, precautions while taking the exam, and perhaps -- for best results -- the help of a counselor or psychologist.

Objective examinations

Standardized objective examinations, such as the Graduate Record Examinations, are moving toward computerization. Bulletins from the testing services, in particular those available from the Education Testing Service (Princeton, NJ 08541), now offer detailed information and recommendations about taking both the paper-and-pencil and the "computer adaptive" versions. Also, there are numerous paperback books about preparing for and taking standardized examinations for graduate and professional schools. Among the most reputable and widely used of these books are Barron's (Barron's Educational Series, Inc.) and Princeton Review (Villard Books).

For most standardized objective tests, as well as for teacher-made objective tests such as those given in many large lecture courses, keep these general points in mind:

1. If you practice answering the types of objective questions likely to be asked, you can improve your performance on the actual test.

2. If you can identify at least one of the choices as wrong, you'll *possibly* be safe in guessing the answer; if you can identify at least two of the choices as wrong, you'll *probably* be safe in guessing the answer.

Here are a few basic recommendations for answering three common types of standardized objective questions more accurately and efficiently. Similar approaches are useful in taking many teacher-made objective tests.

Word opposites

When you take a multiple-choice test that requires choosing word opposites, or antonyms, keep in mind that it takes less time to choose words that are alike, or synonyms.

Think of the given word as changed to its opposite – by adding "not" to a positive word or by cutting the "un-" or "in-" negative prefix from a negative word. Then search among the choices for a word that means the *same* as the word(s) now in your mind. For example, change "laborious" to "not laborious" and you will recognize immediately that "easy" is the best answer.

Sentence completions

1. Read the whole sentence, with blanks.

2. If there are two blanks, decide from the context what the relationship between the words in the two blanks is likely to be (e.g., are the words likely to be similar or opposite in meaning?), then think about the kind of word that might fit the blank that seems easiest to fill.

3. Read the choices for the one blank only, and choose two possible answers from the choices for that blank.

4. Reread the whole sentence twice, filling in the blanks with only the two pairs of answers that you think might be correct. Decide which of the two pairs is better.

Reading comprehension

1. Preview the paragraph(s) by reading:

    a) the first sentence of the first paragraph

    b) the last paragraph

    c) the first and last sentences of any other paragraphs.

2. Read the first two questions without reading the multiple choices.

3. Read the whole selection with these questions in mind.

4. Read the choices for the first two questions, and answer the question.

5. Use appropriate reading approaches to answer the other questions. For example, scan for details, or carefully read a sentence or paragraph in which there is a metaphor that must be explained.

6. To answer questions about inferences or conclusions, select two or three possibilities from the choices. Test each possibility by rereading the paragraph with only one inference in mind. When or if a phrase or sentence seems to contradict

that inference, stop reading the paragraph and start again with another inference in mind.

7. The item you choose should answer the question more accurately and fully than the other choices given – and it should answer the question on the basis of the passage given, rather than on the basis of your own knowledge or opinion.

In order to discover the value of these procedures, and develop the habit of using them, apply them on numerous sample questions given in a reputable book about multiple-choice examinations.

*Part III:
Ways to Improve
Favorable
Attitudes and
Avoid
Unfavorable
Ones*

16

Improving Motivation, Concentration, and Willpower

Motivation, concentration, and willpower—attitudes that are essential for effective and efficient reading and studying—can usually be improved in six basic ways:

1. **Look for opportunities to exercise personal choice in your learning activities.**

    a) Select courses or study groups on the basis of your genuine interest in the subject, the readings, and your knowledge about the instructor. To do this, you will need to find out much more than the mere title and brief description of each course and the name of the instructor. You will need to: 1) examine the syllabus (which is usually available in the department office or World Wide Web site) and the books required/recommended (which are usually available in a particular library or bookstore); 2) ask the opinion of others who have taken part in the same course or group; and 3) visit the first session. Also, visit the first session of alternative courses or groups, with the permission of the instructors, so that you can change to one of these if you're not satisfied with your original choice.

    b) If you are starting out in a new school, talk with an academic advisor about your desire to choose courses based primarily on genuine interest, rather than the need to "get requirements out of the way." Once you feel successful in your new school, you are likely to study more effectively for any required courses that may be of less interest to you.

c) If possible, select courses that permit you some choices in the books you read and the subjects you write about.

2. **Clarify your interests and values in relation to your immediate and long-term goals, personal as well as vocational.**

a) Think about your recent choices and what they indicate about your interests and values.

b) Recall times when you have been thoroughly engrossed in what you were reading or writing. What were the elements that may have contributed to your being motivated and able to concentrate? The subject? Instructor? Book? Group? Environment?

c) Discuss your goals with an academic advisor, psychologist at a counseling service, or personnel at a career planning and placement service.

d) Read both fiction and nonfiction that relates to the career and other goals you have been considering.

e) Seek volunteer or paid experience in the field you have been considering and/or talk at length with individuals who seem to be successful in the field.

3. **Increase your motivation by using strategies that activate your interest, curiosity, and desire to learn about the subject.**

For example:

a) Seek positions, courses, and assignments that provide opportunities for applying what you've learned to problems or subjects you really care about. For this purpose, take advantage of an independent study or research seminar, or the equivalent in your career position.

b) Try to understand why a required course that you are reluctant to take would be of value to you. Discuss this concern with appropriate instructors and academic advisors.

c) Consciously think about the relevance of the subject you're studying to your immediate and long-range purposes. Before starting any new course, paper, or project, jot down or write a paragraph or two about its relevance for you, and add another paragraph of evaluation after you've completed the work.

d) Try to alternate studying independently and studying with others in your subject area. Collaborative study is especially motivating for extroverts, but it can be helpful for almost everyone. It can be in person or by telephone, letter, e-mail, or the Internet. Participation in a good group is likely to generate more critical and creative thought than solo study does.

   — Caution: Ask your instructors to state their policy about collaborative studying. If you have any questions about the policy, ask for clarification. You should assume that collaboration is not permitted on take-home exams.

   — For your study group, choose one to four people who you think are conscientious and compatible, and who would commit themselves to mutual learning and encouragement.

   — Set meetings at regular intervals throughout the semester, including several weeks before exams, so that you will have time to ask your professor any questions that arise in the group.

   — Set specific times to start and end the group study, and limit socializing to before and after these times.

   — Decide how each member is expected to prepare for and participate in the meetings. For example, a person could summarize, explain, or lead a discussion about a specific topic or a specific reading assignment (such as an article on an extended bibliography, or a law or business case), or compose questions that will require critical and creative thinking.

For a full discussion of studying in groups, see Ronald Ronstadt's *The Art of Case Analysis* (3rd ed., Dana Point, CA: Lord, 1994).

4. **Increase your concentration by improving your study conditions.**

a) Figure out the times of day when you are most alert for studying, and try to use those times regularly.

b) Give yourself occasional brief breaks (every hour or so, for ten minutes), in which you move around actively, look at distant rather than close objects, and get a breath of fresh air.

c) Give yourself ample light, without glare, to help prevent eye fatigue, and good ventilation to help you breathe and think better.

d) Free yourself from distractions. (For example, noise – if you cannot prevent or move away from distracting noise, either use medically recommended earplugs, or set up a closer, nondistracting sound such as music without words, or a fan.)

· ·

Try to alternate studying independently and studying with others in your subject area.

e) Find a seat in which you can be comfortable but also alert.

f) Get regular exercise, sufficient and regular sleep, and at least three nourishing (but not heavy) meals a day.

g) Make sure your glasses or contacts are a recent prescription, and wear them.

h) Free yourself from substances that may interfere with concentration, such as alcohol, or other drugs. (If you tend to overuse alcohol or other drugs, seek help from a psychological, psychiatric, or counseling service.)

i) Keep a memo pad handy to note any sudden ideas not directly related to your studying, so that these ideas will be retrievable later but will not be on your mind, where they can distract you.

5. **Study actively and efficiently, using methods like those described in this book.**

By doing so, you can shorten the time in which you must concentrate, motivate yourself, and use your willpower. In summary:

a) Organize your work and budget your time (see chapter 2).

b) Increase your background in the subject matter, which will increase your interest in it (see chapter 6).

c) Preview before reading expository material, then "chunk" the material; chew and swallow one chunk before biting off another (see chapters 3 and 10).

d) If you tend to procrastinate before or after previewing, start reading at the part of the book or article that you find most interesting (see chapters 10 and 18).

e) In starting on a research paper, delay taking notes on what each book says, but do note your own ideas and questions about it immediately. Confirm your plans for the paper with your professor or supervisor before proceeding further (see chapter 9).

6. **Investigate possible psychological as well as physiological causes of inadequate motivation, concentration and willpower.**

    Have you had negative experiences related to a subject you're trying to study? Do you feel ambivalent about committing yourself to a major or degree in the subject or field? Are you afraid of failure? Have you been feeling depressed?

    Have you been overusing any drugs, including caffeine or alcohol? Have you had for many years a problem with concentration or learning? Do you think you might have a learning disability, or a related condition such as Attention Deficit Disorder (ADD)?

    a) Talk with a psychologist or psychiatrist – either at a university counseling or mental health service, or in private practice. The sooner you have a professional evaluation and receive help, the more quickly you're likely to improve.

    b) Read books that can give you insight into your attitudes and behavior. Browse in a bookstore or library, follow up book reviews that appeal to you, and ask librarians, advisors, psychologists, or therapists for specific recommendations of books and articles.

    Here are examples of different kinds of books that can be helpful in improving motivation, concentration, and willpower:

    Bolles, Richard Nelson. *What Color is Your Parachute. A Practical Manual for Job-Hunters and Career-Changers.* Berkeley, CA: Ten Speed Press, 1998 (revised annually).

    Burns, David D. *Feeling Good: The New Mood Therapy.* New York: Avon, 1992.

    Hallowell, E. and Ratey, J. *Driven to Distraction.* New York: Simon & Schuster, 1995.

    ———. *Answers to Distraction.* New York: Bantam, 1996.

Pauk, Walter. *How to Study in College*, 6th ed. Boston: Houghton Mifflin, 1997. Sections on "Managing Stress" and "Learning to Concentrate."

Now in order to gain a greater facility of attention we may observe these rules:
1. "Get a good liking to the study or knowledge you would pursue." We may observe that there is not much difficulty in confining the mind to contemplate what we have a great desire to know....
2. "Do not choose your constant place of study by the finery of the prospects, or the most various and entertaining scenes of sensible things." Too much light, or a variety or objects which strike the eye or the ear, especially while they are ever in motion or often changing, have a natural and powerful tendency to steal away the mind too often from its steady pursuit of any subject which we contemplate....

Isaac Watts, 1741

The less interested and motivated you feel towards a particular course or reading assignment, the more you should try to follow the recommendations in this book that are beyond the basic principles of interest and motivation.

As you try a few of the recommendations, you are likely to experience one small success after another. Each success will increase your confidence and relieve your anxiety, and so improve your motivation, concentration, and willpower.

If you follow the recommendations in this guide and find that you don't progress as much or as rapidly as you had anticipated, arrange for an interview about your reading, writing, and studying needs at a university reading/writing improvement service or learning resource center.

17

What to Avoid: Self-Defeating Tendencies

This book is written largely from a positive point of view—it describes what you should try to do in order to learn more in less time. This section is written from the opposite point of view—it emphasizes what you should be careful NOT to do.

There are three main tendencies you should avoid:

Tendency #1: Various forms of procrastination

Procrastination is the number one problem for many students, whatever their level of study. Here, procrastination means putting off the reading, writing, and thinking that you need to do.

1. **Putting off reading and writing**

   You will find in many sections of this book suggestions for ways to overcome procrastination, as well as ways to improve concentration, willpower, and other helpful attitudes. Here are some of those earlier suggestions restated briefly:

   a) Increase your interest in what you're studying:

      (1) Seek opportunities for choices in your courses or study groups and in your assignments (see chapter 16).

(2) Develop your background in the subject (see chapter 7).

(3) Start your reading, after previewing, at the parts of the material that interest you the most (see chapter 16).

b) Whenever you have a major task that you're tempted to procrastinate about, list all the parts that you must include, and start work on the part that is most interesting or motivating to you at the moment (see chapter 18).

c) During the early parts of your task, use methods that will make later parts easier for you. For example, whenever ideas occur to you about a project, make notes of them on index cards or memo pages and file them. You'll be less likely to procrastinate about the project because you'll find satisfaction in organizing and developing further the ideas about it you've accumulated so thoughtfully for yourself.

Sometimes what might seem to be procrastination could more accurately and happily be called postponement. Postponement might be justified when you have more pressing tasks to work on, or when you are sure you will have a better time and place to do the work, or a better state of mind or health.

If you've read many other parts of this book, you'll recognize that previewing, selecting, chunking, and deep processing—the basic steps recommended throughout—are involved in the suggestions outlined above.

2. Putting off thinking

In reading, procrastination may take the form of just opening the book and trying to concentrate on the first page, word by word. Often it takes the form of continually underlining or highlighting the material, which is usually a way of telling yourself that you need to learn these parts eventually – but you don't feel like learning them now.

I've asked many thousands of students how they read for their courses, and most of them have answered in approximately these words: "I put off the reading as long as possible. Finally, I open the book and try to concentrate on the first page. As I go along, slowly, I highlight with a yellow marker. I often highlight too much, because I have trouble deciding what's important." The student usually pauses here, and I have to ask, "When you come to the end of the chapter, what do you do?" He looks puzzled, shrugs his shoulders, and says, "I close the book and move on to something else."

These students tend to not think carefully about what they read until they have to answer questions from others about the material. By that time they are likely to remember very little about it. Their highlighting just tells them that their eyes once moved across those lines of print.

Similarly, in note-taking from listening, procrastination may take the form of mechanically putting every word on paper. When students fail to make notes selectively and to include their own immediate questions or ideas about the material, and when they fail to review or think further about the notes within 24 hours after taking them, they have missed pleasurable as well as dependable ways to learn more in less time.

If you tend to procrastinate, try applying the suggestions mentioned in item 1 above and in other sections of this book. If you still have procrastination problems, talk with a counselor or psychologist about some of the personal factors that might be involved.

Tendency #2: Overly passive reading and studying

Overly passive reading and studying means there is little or no critical or creative thinking involved.

Some of the methods of reading and studying described above as forms of procrastination are also examples of overly passive study. Other examples are the arduous ways that some students read and study for exams. They have told me, "I recopy my class notes, and I take so many notes from my reading that it's almost like recopying the books," or "At exam time, I go over all my class notes, and I reread all the chapter assignments."

Statements like these have convinced me that many students haven't been taught better strategies for learning or, if they have been taught, they haven't become sufficiently convinced of the value of these strategies to try using them. They persist in the rituals of highlighting books or recopying notes, which take too much time for the little they accomplish.

Studying better doesn't necessarily mean studying more or longer; on the contrary, procrastinating and then studying too passively takes more time and leads to less-satisfying results. To read and study more actively, try the following:

1. **Think critically and creatively about what you're reading, writing, or studying.**

2. **Discuss what you're learning with your professor and teaching assistants, your study group members, and pen or e-mail pals.**

3. **Apply appropriately what you've learned.**

These and other methods described in this book can help you integrate new concepts and terminology into your knowledge system and help you feel more confident, competent, and motivated to learn well.

Tendency #3: Intellectual dishonesty

Among the central purposes of education and professional work are the pursuit of truth and knowledge, self-realization, helping others, and improving society. These purposes are contradicted or subverted when the means taken toward them are dishonest or unethical – cheating, failing to acknowledge sources adequately, plagiarizing, misrepresenting records, or contributing to the dishonest or unethical methods of others.

Some students may resort to intellectual dishonesty because they don't realize that its various forms can be easily recognized by instructors, who have a professional responsibility to act on their recognition. Some students also may not realize that punishment for intellectual dishonesty can include a failing grade for the academic work involved or for the whole course, and a judicial record of academic misconduct, suspension, and/or dismissal.

In many cases, students and professionals may be tempted to cheat because they feel desperate as a result of procrastination and poor planning. If you find yourself in this situation, you should immediately talk with an advisor about effective ways to cope with your pressing problem (such as requesting an extension of time); seek instruction in time management, including more efficient ways to work or study; and seek personal counseling.

For more information about this subject, see Appendix A.

Part IV:
Ways to Read
and Learn Well
and with
Pleasure –
Lifelong

18

Keeping Up in Your Profession

You have graduated from college and perhaps from graduate or professional school, and you are beginning to work in your new job or profession. You know that keeping up with current knowledge in your field and related disciplines is a professional responsibility that not only makes you better at what you do, but also makes you more interested in it and enthusiastic about it. Yet how can you work in a demanding profession, keep up with current knowledge in and beyond your immediate areas of responsibility, and also lead a reasonably balanced life? Keeping up is difficult to manage, but it will be easier and take less time if you go about it in an organized way.

When you are working in your field, you will be keeping up with specific aspects related to your immediate responsibilities. To keep up in your field more broadly and efficiently, you will need to use strategies like these, adapting them to your particular profession and style:

1. **Through universities, libraries and bookstores, professional organizations, and publishers in your field, find authorities and consult them frequently.**

    a) Universities, libraries, and bookstores:

        1) Browse in university and specialized bookstores that stock books for courses in your field and closely related fields. In each book that looks useful, scan the index for topics of particular interest to you, read the table of contents, and preview

chapters of immediate interest. This can help you keep up, as well as decide what to buy.

2) Examine the syllabi of courses in your field or related fields, and choose one or more courses to take or audit.

3) With the help of a reference librarian, make a computerized search for summaries of articles on a subject of your professional interest. Reading the summaries can give you a good overview of information and materials available on the subject, and help you decide confidently which materials to locate and read more fully.

4) Examine a "current awareness" publication regularly; for example, *Current Contents* (published by the Institute for Scientific Information, Philadelphia) reprints the tables of contents of current journals in various fields – Current Contents for Social and Behavioral Sciences, Life Sciences, Arts and Humanities, Engineering, Technology and Applied Science, and Physical, Chemical, and Earth Sciences.

5) Clip or photocopy reviews of books that you might want to buy.

b) Professional organizations:

1) Join one or more professional organizations, at least for a year's trial. Some organizations have reduced rates for the first year or for student members.

2) Subscribe to at least one journal published by each organization that you join; attend some of the organizations' seminars, conferences, or conventions; and buy some books and tapes that they make available.

3) If you cannot attend a conference you are interest-

ed in, ask the sponsors for a program, and occasionally write to speakers requesting copies of presentations or any materials distributed.

4) Submit articles of your own to journals of professional organizations, or prepare presentations for their conferences.

c) Publishers:

1) Browse through catalogs of publishing companies in your field, note books for possible ordering, and request that your name be added to the publishers' mailing lists.

2) Save time and avoid errors in purchasing books by browsing in the publishers' exhibits that are part of many professional conventions and placing orders there for books you have examined.

3) Buy a current dictionary or handbook for your field.

2. Prepare to keep up with your reading by previewing and selecting.

a) When you add a book or a journal to your library, or borrow one from a friend in your field or from a library, take a few minutes to prepare to read it. In the table of contents, if the book is your own, make a short line or question mark next to each chapter or article that you think you want to read soon. If you have borrowed the book, photocopy the title page, copyright notice, and table of contents so that you can mark them freely and save them for future reference.

b) As soon as possible, preview sections, chapters, or articles of immediate interest to get a sense of their scope and quality and to satisfy your curiosity temporarily. Make an X by any articles or chapters that you think are not worth reading further.

c) If you want to remember what you previewed, tell yourself or a companion about it from memory before moving on.

d) When you expect to travel or have some other appropriate time for reading professional material, take with you the books or journals that you have previewed and selected.

3. **Make notes appropriate for your purposes.**

a) When you read, make notes according to the methods outlined in chapters 5 and 7.

b) Write the notes in any of several places, according to how or where you want to store your notes: at the top of the first page of the article or chapter, on the flyleaf, on index cards, or on 81/2-by-11-inch paper. Two of the advantages of making most of your notes on separate cards or pages, rather than in the books or journals themselves, are that the books will be more readable without distracting marks (for you and others who may read them in the future), and that you will still have the notes if you give away, lend, or lose the book.

c) Note a reminder of your overall judgment of each chapter or article by appropriate marks in the margins of the table of contents; for example, by checks: √, √–, or √+. Writing symbols in the table of contents can be helpful to you immediately and at many points in your professional future, up to the day when you decide to give away some of the books and journals you have accumulated through the years. All you will need to do is look for a √+ on the cover or the table of contents to decide whether you should keep the material.

d) In the margins of the table of contents, next to the titles of the portions you have read, write the page numbers and parts of pages you found especially valuable.

e) Photocopy pages that you must keep readily accessible. Also photocopy the title page, copyright notice, and table of contents, or note complete bibliographic information directly on the first or last page of each copy; you will need this information later if you want to cite the material or write for permission to use it. (See Appendix B for information about copyright laws.) Determine the key word or subject under which you should file the pages, and file them in alphabetized accordion-files, in indexed file folders, or in your computer.

4. **If you have accumulated quantities of books and journals but have given them little more than a glance, bring yourself to read them by previewing, chunking, and selecting.**

a) Preview and chunk: Look over all the books, group them by the subjects of concern to you, and subgroup them alphabetically by author.

· ·

Begin reading at the part that appeals to you most.

b) Preview and select: Preview a few books that particularly appeal to you, and select one of these to start reading as thoroughly as necessary. Begin reading at the part that appeals to you most, thus lessening any tendency you may have to procrastinate. Having started so well, you might feel inspired to move on to the next most appealing part, or to go back and read from the beginning, or to move on to a different book.

c) When you encounter a part that you especially want to remember, tell yourself or a companion about it from memory.

d) Keep a loose-leaf memo book in your pocket or pocketbook, one with pages the same size as the index cards you use regularly, so that you can note new ideas, information, or references immediately and can file the notes easily.

5. File your notes and photocopies systematically, for ready retrieval.

Browse in a well-stocked stationery or office-supply store and buy various kinds of aids to filing, like these:

a) for short-term storage when you are in a hurry, large accordion notebooks or envelopes, with alphabetic tabs, and file boxes with index cards and dividers;

b) for long-term storage when you have time to file more carefully, containers of various types and sizes with self-stick labels – shelves, file drawers and cabinets, three-ring notebooks with dividers that have pockets;

c) for longest-term storage when you want the materials to remain in good condition for as long as possible, acid-free containers, which are available through companies that sell archival material (museum or library personnel can refer you to these companies).

6. Exchange information and ideas with colleagues.

a) Participate in continuing education, which may be provided through your workplace.

b) Initiate continuing education. For example, organize a discussion group for interested members of your profession and related fields.

c) Meet colleagues for lunch and informal exchange of information and ideas – including ideas about keeping up in your field or profession.

d) Communicate by telephone or letter, or by e-mail or the Internet, if you can't meet in person.

7. **If and when you decide to change fields, cut back to part-time, or retire, enjoy additional fruits of lifelong learning.**

a) Give away or sell books and journals that you no longer need and that others might find helpful.

   1) If you haven't marked all over your books, they will be more readable by others, so that you can sell them or trade them, give them to friends, or contribute them (with an income tax deduction) to professional libraries. Some institutions have sibling institutions, often ones in developing countries, for which gifts of books are welcome. An office of planned giving or international programs in the benefactor institution may take care of shipping the books.

   2) If you decide to give away large numbers of books and journals, employ a librarian to list and assess them. Copies of such an assessment can give you an accurate record of your gift's value for income tax deductions; they can make your gift more useful to the institution to which you give them; and they can remind you of which books and journals you gave away, if you start looking for one in its former place in your library.

b) If you audit courses, join reading groups, or read extensively on your own, continue using methods that have helped you learn more in less time. Or you may simply want to enjoy reading without concern for how much you remember. More and more you may agree with Sir Francis Bacon in his essay "Of Studies": "Some books are to be tasted, others to be swallowed, and some few to be chewed and digested."

19

Keeping Better Informed Through Newspapers and Magazines

Keeping up with new information in your professional field, like keeping up with school assignments, is a major responsibility. You also have to keep well-informed for all the other roles you have, from family member to voter to volunteer. For all these responsibilities, there are many ways to learn more in less time.

Keeping yourself well-informed can seem like a never-ending chore or a pleasurable challenge, depending upon your attitude and the way you go about it. Educating yourself for the many purposes in your life usually requires more than reading head-lines, skimming a few articles, listening to National Public Radio or other news-centered radio stations, and watching televised information programs. It requires continual and selective reading, discussing, storing, and reviewing.

Here are some ways to keep better informed and to feel less over-whelmed by all the new information that seems important to know and remember:

Read newspapers and magazines selectively

1. **Evaluate the periodicals that you have been reading regularly.**

In addition to a local newspaper, do these periodicals include at least one other major newspaper and several different types of periodicals? Browse through a well-stocked periodical collection of a library or bookstore to find additional periodicals you might want to explore.

2. **To develop and satisfy new interests, keep adding and subtracting periodicals to read regularly.**

   For example, if you become more concerned about maintaining your health, add a health newsletter, like the *University of California at Berkeley Wellness Letter,* or *Nutrition Action Health Letter,* published by the Center for Science in the Public Interest.

3. **Make some effort to impress upon your memory what you have read.**

   The process can be like the ways you remember pleasant events or vacations. On vacations you may take photographs, write postcards or letters, keep a journal, or bring home souvenirs. Later, you review your mementos and so refresh your memory and deepen your insights about your experiences. Similarly, to keep better informed about subjects of interest to you, save articles or whole issues of magazines and review them later.

4. **To remember more of the information you have read, follow appropriate steps for previewing, selecting, chunking, and processing.**

   These steps are described in chapters 10 and 6.

5. **As you engage in your work or other activities, consciously try to apply what you have learned from any material that you have read to keep informed.**

   This will help you integrate the information more fully into your knowledge system and help you retrieve it more quickly when you need it.

Preview and select

1. **When you start reading a newspaper, look at the first page to get an idea of the main news and features.**

    If you don't have time to read all the sections immediately, look over the pages quickly, check the articles you want to read, and mark on the top of the first page of each section the pages where the articles you've checked appear.

2. **When you pick up a magazine, browse through the pages and mark in the margin of the table of contents the articles that you want to read.**

3. **Preview any article of interest to you, then read the article selectively if you decide you want to know more than you gained from the preview alone.**

Select and chunk

When you are reading an article, bracket in the margin any lines or paragraphs of particular interest to you. If the article seems to you worth saving, note the number of the article's first page (like this, p. 9+) on the front page of the newspaper, or on the cover or table of contents of the magazine. If you took this step when you first browsed through the newspaper, circle the page number after you have read the article and have decided to save it.

1. **When you have finished reading a whole magazine or a whole section of a newspaper, mark a check (√) on the front of those you want to keep, and mark an X on any that you do not want to keep.**

    Then, when trash or recycle day comes, you will not have to spend time deciding which magazines and newspapers to discard or save.

2. **Carefully tear out pages that include articles you want to read when you have more time.**

Collect them in a well-marked and sturdy folder that is easy to carry.

Process deeply

1. **After you have read and marked an article, review immediately, from memory, whatever information you want to be sure to remember.**

   To remember the information better and longer, tell someone else about what you have read, and discuss issues or questions raised in the material.

2. **Develop a simple method for storing articles or magazines for a period of months.**

   After many months, choose from your collection any materials that you think are worth keeping on file for years. This process can help you remember what you learned from all the articles, as well as help you make special articles accessible for future use.

Store selected articles short-term or long-term

1. **Before discarding a newspaper or magazine, look at the page numbers you've noted on the front page, cover, or table of contents.**

   Tear out any pages you have noted that still seem worth keeping and store them in a box or drawer. At this point, don't spend time clipping out the articles from the pages. If there are any magazines that you want to save whole, put them aside on a special shelf.

2. **At the top of your pile of newspaper and magazine pages or in a file drawer, keep folders for collecting articles on a few subjects of greatest interest to you, such as health, travel, or new books.**

This rough categorizing can save you time in several ways: it will make it easier to find an article about your main interests, and it will prevent you from accumulating too large a pile of unsorted articles.

3. **Wait a year or so to clip out some of the articles.**

By then, you can decide quickly which articles you still want, and probably more than half of them will not seem worth saving any longer.

4. **Your attitude about this whole process can affect how easy or difficult it seems.**

If you think of it as a way to refresh your memory, it will seem pleasant rather than tedious. If you think of it as part of an overall effort to keep better informed, you will not be so inclined to procrastinate. Starting with the following steps will help, too:

a) Gather the supplies you will need: file folders and an accordion file, a trash basket, labels, scissors, a stapler, transparent tape for any torn pages, a colored pen, and your memorandum book or calendar.

b) Start clipping and filing from the group or pile of articles that has the most immediate priority or value for you. For example, you might want to retrieve articles on an aspect of health that is of particular importance to you.

c) Review the marked parts of each article, reconsidering their possible value for you or others. For all articles that you decide to save, write the name and date of the periodical on the first page, if this information is not already printed there.

d) File these articles in an accordion file-folder. Develop a table of contents for the file-folder and store it inside. Set aside any articles that you want to photocopy and/or share with others.

e) In the year or so after a clipping-and-filing session,

whenever you need specific material that you placed temporarily in the accordion file, transfer to a file folder the whole group of articles on that subject, for long-term storage in your home or office. In other words, transfer the articles from quick and temporary storage to long-term storage, one subject at a time, rather than attempting to file permanently all the materials about all the subjects at once!

f) For articles in whole magazines that you save, mark on the table of contents the page numbers and parts of pages ("87 B," or "90 E") that you think are especially valuable (see chapter 5). If the periodical provides an annual index of articles, mark in the index the articles you found most valuable.

·······························

The whole process may become a kind of hobby for you.

Adapt your methods to your evolving interests and needs

As your interests and needs change, revise and reorganize your collection of articles:

1. **Subcategorize your files and revise your tables of contents accordingly.**

    If you realize that your main interests are health and travel, subcategorize these topics: divide "health" into subcategories like "nutrition" and "safety," and divide "travel" into subcategories, such as different places you want to go.

    a) For a subject like "travel," keep folders handy for filing material about the trips you're planning currently. Keep other travel material with files that you use less frequently.

b) Use a notebook with dividers that have pockets to store brochures and other material about some subjects, such as nearby places of interest, restaurants, and places to stay.

2. **Compile a table of contents for all your files and note where you've stored the files.**

3. **If you decide to do extensive research to keep yourself better informed about a subject, you can use the same methods that you have developed for your professional needs.**

For example, borrow or buy books on the subject, and arrange for a computer search for more articles.

Why bother with a system to keep yourself informed?

1. Your personal collection of articles, with your brackets and written comments, is a record of your particular interests, concerns, and tastes. It's not impersonal, like a printout of abstracts from a computer search of articles. (However, a printout of abstracts can be a useful addition to your collection, if you mark it up for your purposes.)

2. Reviewing your articles, when you weed out and store them, is a valuable way to remember them longer, because the process involves both ego and pleasure. It's like taking photographs when you are on vacation, then later sorting and mounting them. In fact, the whole process may become a kind of hobby for you.

3. Saving selected articles gives you a ready resource to tap for your many roles or purposes.

4. As you mark and save articles, you may realize that you are developing new interests and values, which can lead you to affiliate with new groups, enjoy new hobbies, or even explore new careers.

20

Getting More Pleasure from Reading

Many people haven't developed a habit or hobby of reading for pleasure and satisfaction as well as for knowledge. Some people, even those with high levels of education, rarely read more than a daily newspaper and the periodicals essential to their livelihood. Recommendations in chapters 18 and 19 can help you enjoy such reading more fully. Recommendations in chapter 16 can also help you increase your pleasure in various kinds of reading, writing, and studying.

Here are some basic ways to find more pleasure and satisfaction in reading – and thus increase your desire to read more.

Let your interest lead you to reading

— Your genuine interest is the most helpful guide to reading for pleasure. Choose books on subjects you really care about or find appealing, perhaps books related to a concern or an experience in your personal life, or to a film or television program you keep thinking about. Look for the best available books on the subject. Get help from book reviews and from book-loving friends, librarians, and booksellers.

— If you want to warm up to a book, play, poem or author that appeals to you but seems intimidating, locate a recording of the work. Follow along in the book as you listen to a good reading or dramatization of it. You may enjoy the book so much that you'll want to read parts of it again on your own.

— If a book recommended to you seems only moderately interesting, increase your interest and pleasure by developing more background for it. Try reading something short or easy about the subject or the author. Look for a favorable experience that can give you more understanding and feeling about the topic or the writer. For example, if you can't get far in reading *Moby Dick,* read about Herman Melville and whales in a good encyclopedia, or put the book aside until you can visit Mystic Seaport, Connecticut, an authentic restored whaling village, or visit the area near Pittsfield, Massachusetts, where Melville lived at the time he wrote the book.

Preview and select

— When you have several books to choose from, start with the book that you feel most motivated to read. If that book is nonfiction, start reading at the part that interests you most. If the book is fiction, read the first chapter before deciding when or whether to continue reading.

— In whatever book you choose, continue to read the parts selectively, if you like. Feel free to read some parts quickly, some parts thoroughly. Many people are reluctant readers because they feel they have to start at the beginning of every book and read every word.

Process the material as you please

Read as actively as you like:

— You can just read, expecting that your interest and emotional involvement will help you appreciate and absorb the material.

— Or you can take simple and pleasurable steps to help you

enjoy and remember the book in other ways. Make a note of the pages you find most worthwhile and write down your thoughts and feelings about them. Use paper separate from the book, so that you have plenty of space for writing. Or, if the book is your own, write on the flyleaf or table of contents so that you can photocopy your notes easily before you lend it or give it away. Think of your notes as similar to the photographs or sketches that you make when you're on vacation, and that you look at when you want to refresh your memory and renew your pleasure.

— Whatever way you read the book, think of its relevance to your life and the world, and discuss it with others – in person or by telephone, letter, or e–mail. You'll be enhancing your memories of the book and extending the pleasures of reading.

If necessary, let more than interest keep you reading for pleasure

— If you feel tense as you read, or impatient to stop, one of the causes might be eye fatigue or eye strain. You might need to have better light for reading, or you might need to be examined by an ophthalmologist for a newer prescription of glasses or contact lenses.

— If you need more structure or more socializing to help you read more, enroll in a promising course or study group.

— Consider the ways that various kinds of reading might help you achieve some of your goals.

— Gain more confidence, competence, and pleasure in reading by getting help from an adult-learning specialist. Make an appointment or request a referral at a learning resource center in a high school, college, or university.

— For more ideas about getting more pleasure from reading, see "Reading fiction or poetry for full effect and meaning," in chapter 6, and "Taking notes from poetry in a first course in literature," in chapter 7.

Gradually, you may realize that, like countless fortunate people in every generation, you've found recreation and release, stimulation and wonder, beauty and delight in reading for pleasure, and you'll want to make it a frequent and permanent part of your life.

Your genuine interest is the most helpful guide to reading for pleasure.

Bibliography

The following books are recommended as additional sources of ideas or encouragement for improving reading, writing, and studying. See also the bibliographies in chapters 6, 13, and 16.

These books are likely to be available in libraries, university bookstores, and some general bookstores. If not, bookstores may order them for you, or you may order them directly by calling the publisher's 800 number (obtainable by dialing information, 800-555-1212).

Barnet, Sylvan. *A Short Guide to Writing About Art*, 5th ed. New York: Watson–Guptill, 1996.

Gibaldi, Joseph, and Walter S. Achtert, eds. *MLA Handbook for Writers of Research Papers, Theses and Dissertations*, 4th ed. New York: Modern Language Association, 1995.

Mann, Thomas. *A Guide to Library Research Methods*. New York: Oxford University Press, 1990.

Pauk, Walter. *How to Study in College,* 6th ed. Boston: Houghton Mifflin, 1997.

Publication Manual of the American Psychological Association, 4th ed. Washington, D.C.: American Psychological Association, 1994.

Ronstadt, Ronald. *The Art of Case Analysis: A Guide to the Diagnosis of Business Situations*, 3rd ed. Dana Point, CA: Lord, 1994.

Turabian, Kate L. *A Manual for Writers of Term Papers, Theses, and Dissertations,* 6th ed. Chicago: University of Chicago Press, 1996.

Vogel, S. and Adelman, P. *Success for College Students with Learning Disabilities*. New York: Springer-Verlag, 1992, reprinted 1994.

Appendix A.

Progress in Helping Students Avoid Self-Defeating Tendencies

1. More and more teachers—in secondary schools, undergraduate and graduate education, and professional and continuing education—are helping students to learn more in less time and to avoid self-defeating tendencies such as procrastination, overly passive study, and intellectual dishonesty.

They are doing this by:

— providing for greater student interest, especially by providing more choices in assignments

— describing and demonstrating their own methods of study and time management in their fields

— encouraging critical and creative thinking

— facilitating and delimiting group study, especially by describing in the syllabus and discussing in class (a) types of aid or collaboration recommended and the types not allowed in the course, and (b) ways to acknowledge in print any aid or collaboration on work submitted for evaluation

—referring students for appropriate support services.

2. More advisors, coaches, and counseling psychologists are informing students about academic support services available, and encouraging students to use them early and regularly.

3. More supervisors, continuing-education administrators, librarians, and booksellers are informing professionals and business people about resources that can help them manage their time, keep up in their fields, and enjoy lifelong learning.

4. More administrators, in collaboration with instructors and students, are:

— developing codes of intellectual integrity

— publishing the codes of intellectual integrity along with descriptive lists of academic support services available, and thus informing students positively about what they are expected to do, while also informing them about what they are expected NOT to do

— including in their published information reminders of ways to protect computer files from misuse by others, such as using log-in names that are impossible to guess, and putting safety blocks on computer files

— allowing students to have an active role in developing and maintaining the judicial system

— including among the consequences of intellectual dishonesty not only appropriate punishment but also appropriate assistance to prevent recurrence. Punishment may include a failing grade for a paper or exam or for the whole course, a judicial record of academic misconduct, suspension, or dismissal. Assistance would include instruction and counseling to help students become more competent and confident in their work and therefore less likely to be intellectually dishonest again.

5. Much of the progress in these areas is the result of (a) increased collaboration among instructors and the staffs of academic support services, and (b) wider dissemination of articles and books on enhancing learning, such as *Teaching Tips: Strategies, Research, and Theory for College and University Teachers,* by Wilbert J. McKeachie et al. (9th ed. Lexington, MA: D. C. Heath, 1994).

All these efforts, and the favorable response of students and professionals, promise to reduce procrastination, overly passive reading, and intellectual dishonesty, and so to increase learning and improve individual lives and society.

Appendix B.

Copyright Law: An Increasing Concern of Students and Professionals

The main purpose of copyright laws has been to protect the rights of authors and artists and their publishers, for the ultimate benefit of the public. In the United States, the first federal copyright law, which was enacted by Congress in 1790, emphasized authors. It protected books, maps, and charts against printing, reprinting, publishing, and vending by unauthorized persons. Over the years, additional classes of works have been added and exclusive rights have been expanded.

The doctrine of Fair Use, which originated in the 1840s, limits the rights of authors, artists, and publishers by allowing certain kinds of copying that are not considered infringements of the law. The current interpretation of Fair Use and a few other provisions of recent copyright laws are explained briefly in the excerpts below, from Harry G. Henn's *Henn on Copyright Law: A Practitioner's Guide*, 3rd ed. (New York: Practising Law Institute, 1991).

Careful avoidance of unauthorized copying or copyright infringement has become even more important because, in March of 1989, the United States finally joined the Bern Union (Union Internationale pour la Protection des Œuvres Littéraires et Artistiques). This is a hundred-year-old international union of more than sixty countries, with headquarters in Bern, Switzerland. Each country belonging to the union grants citizens of other member countries the same copyright privileges as its own citizens. Although the United States has not acceded to all the provisions of the Bern convention, copyright law will be increasingly significant, in view of the added protection afforded to authors and publishers, when a country becomes a signatory to the Bern convention.

It should not be overlooked that copyright law protects only original expression, not facts, regardless of how much effort was made to locate the facts. The Supreme Court of the United States, in an important decision in March 1991, held:

> *Facts, whether alone or as part of a compilation, are not original and therefore may not be copyrighted. A factual compilation is eligible for copyright if it features an original selection or arrangement of facts, but the copyright is limited to the particular selection or arrangement. In no event may copyright extend to the facts themselves.*

For more information about current copyright law in the United States, write or call the Copyright Office in the Library of Congress, to request its free packet of informational materials (which, like all U.S. Government materials, are not copyrighted). The address of the Copyright Office is 101 Independence Avenue SE, Washington, DC 20559; the telephone number is 202-707-3000. If you need specific legal advice, especially about copying material created by citizens of countries other than your own, consult an attorney.

When in doubt about using any copyrighted material, always write to the publisher for permission to copy it at least three months in advance of when you need to use it. Be sure to describe or list the pages you want to copy, your intended audience, and your purposes. The permissions editor will tell you whether or not you can have permission to copy the material, in what form the acknowledgment must be given, and the fee, if any.

I am indebted to Arthur H. Seidel, Esq., for most of this information about copyright law, and for his assistance in obtaining my copyright for all five editions of this book.

The following are excerpts from *Henn on Copyright Law: A Practitioner's Guide*, 3rd ed., by Harry G. Henn (New York: Practising Law Institute, 1991):

Fair use

In general

The 1976 Act provided no definition of fair use [one of the exceptions to the copyright law], but suggests criteria. Whether a use is fair depends upon:

1. The "purpose" of the use; and

2. At least four "factors."

Purposes

Use can be "fair" for "purposes" "such as" criticism, comment, news, reporting, teaching (including multiple copies for classroom use), scholarship, or research. [pp. 227–229]

Factors

In determining whether the use "in any particular case" is a fair use, the "factors" to be considered shall "include":

1. The "purpose" and "character" of the use, including whether such use is of a "commercial nature" or is "for nonprofit educational purposes";

2. The "nature" of the copyrighted work;

3. The "amount and substantiality of the portion used" in relation to the copyrighted work as a whole; and

4. The effect of the use upon the "potential market for or value of" the copyrighted work. . . . [pp. 230–231]

This fourth factor, "the effect of the use upon the potential market for or value of the copyrighted work," "is undoubtedly the single most important element of fair use." [p. 234]

Classroom copying of books and periodicals

The guidelines for classroom copying in not-for-profit educational institutions with respect to books and periodicals were prepared by representatives of the Ad Hoc Committee of

Educational Institutions and Organizations on Copyright Law
Revision, the Authors League of America, Inc., and the
Association of American Publishers, Inc. Although not binding,
the guidelines significantly influence courts, and have the practical
impact of statutory provisions.

Single copies

A teacher may reproduce a single copy, subject to "prohibitions,"
for research or teaching purposes, of:

1. A chapter from a book;

2. An article from a periodical or newspaper;

3. A short story, short essay, or short poem, whether or not from
a collective work;

4. A chart, graph, diagram, drawing, cartoon, or picture from a
book, periodical, or newspaper. [p. 237]

Multiple copies

A teacher may make multiple copies for classroom use if the
copying meets certain tests for brevity, spontaneity, and cumula-
tive effect. Each copy must also include a notice of copyright. [pp.
237–238]

Prohibitions

Prohibitions applicable to both single and multiple copying are:

1. The copies may not be used for anthologies, compilations, or
collective works;

2. "Consumable" materials, such as workbooks, tests, and
answer sheets, may not be copied;

3. Copying may not be used to substitute for purchasing, be
"directed by higher authority," or be repeated "with respect to
the same item by the same teacher from term to term";

4. The student may not be charged more than the actual costs of
the photocopying. [pp. 238–239]

Reproduction and distribution by libraries and archives

Conditions

The rights of reproduction and distribution of a library or archives, or any of its employees acting within the scope of their employment, are limited to "no more than one copy or phonorecord of a work" and are subject to three specified overall conditions: [p. 250]

1. The making must be "without any purpose of direct or indirect commercial advantage";

2. The collections of the library or archives must be open to the public or available not only to affiliated researchers but also to other persons "doing research in a specialized field"; and

3. The reproduction or distribution must include a "notice of copyright." [p. 251]

Liability of user of reproducing equipment or requester of copies or phonorecords

Liability for copyright infringement of a person who uses the reproducing equipment in a library or archive or who requests copies or phonorecords of articles or other contributions to a copyrighted collection or periodical issue or of a small part of any other copyrighted work for any such act, or for any later use of such copy or phonorecord, if it exceeds fair use, is not excused by the libraries-and-archives provisions. [pp. 260–261]

Future prospects

There are growing disputes between publishers and authors, on the one hand, and librarians and educators, on the other.

A private Copyright Clearance Center (CCC) was established in 1978 to collect fees from photocopiers and to divide the proceeds among copyright owners. In 1984, the Center began to issue blanket licenses under a contract fee based on statistical samples

for periodicals and journals ("Annual Authorization Service").
As a result, increased numbers of corporations have subscribed.
[p. 263]